Revelations for the Soul

By

Bishop John C. Parks

Th.D., BS. MBA, ESPO

Revelations for the Soul

Library of Congress

Cataloging-in-Publication Data

Paperback ISBN: 978-8-89397-382-2

Hardcover ISBN: 979-8-89397-383-9

Library of Congress Card Catalog Number

1-14712745641

Published by

Bookwave Publishing

Manufactured in the United States of America

Acknowledgments

First, I give all glory, honor, and praise to God, whose infinite wisdom and grace have guided me through every step of this journey. Without His calling and presence in my life, this book would not exist.

To those who recognized and affirmed the value of God's calling on my life—your encouragement has been a light in moments of doubt and a strength in seasons of growth. Your belief in me, your prayers, and your unwavering support have been pivotal in this work coming to fruition.

The most challenging part of a book is to write the acknowledgments. So many people make a book a reality—any attempt to name all the people who have affected my 49 years of ministry is challenging. I am incredibly fortunate to have had so many beautiful people for over four decades, of many who supported, encouraged, and even pushed me in extraordinary ways. So, instead, let me thank God for everyone who has worked to enrich my life. Thank you for your thoughtfulness, support, and, most of all, your prayers. I have met people worldwide who inspire, listen to, teach, and encourage me to remain steadfast amid life's vicissitudes. I sincerely appreciate you because you are a catalyst for helping me to grow as a pastor, teacher, father, and Saint of God.

In the select category that demands mention are the following persons. I want to thank Tameica Lightbourne of Nassau Bahamas, who encouraged me to use all my spiritual gifts. Thank you. In addition, I would like to give special thanks to Bishop Ian Keith Brathwaite, Sr., and Prophetess Koralee Brathwaite, Senior Pastor and Prophetess of the Bread of Life Baptist Church of Nassau, Bahamas, for moving mountains and helping me solidify connecting with certain persons of distinction in Nassau, Bahamas, over the past twenty-six years to this day. I give distinction to the Honorable His Grace, Phillip "Brave' Davis, Prime Minister of the Commonwealth of the Bahamas, for such an inspiring foreword.

To my friends and those in my faith community who have spoken life into me and encouraged me to keep pressing forward, your words have been a balm to my soul and a testament to God's power working through His people.

Finally, to every reader of this book, I pray that these revelations inspire you to draw closer to God and embrace His calling in your life. May you find the same hope, joy, and peace He has graciously poured into me.

With gratitude and love,
Bishop John C. Parks

Table of Contents

FOREWORD _____ 1

THE AUTHOR'S PREFACE _____ 2

CHAPTER 1: THE WAKE-UP CALL _____ 4

CHAPTER 2: GOD'S PRIMARY CONCERN OUR SOUL _____ 13

CHAPTER 3: GOING BEYOND PRAISE TO INTIMACY WITH GOD _____ 33

CHAPTER 4: GOD'S PURPOSE FOR REVELATIONS _____ 39

CHAPTER 5: IT'S ALL ABOUT HOW YOU READ IT _____ 45

CHAPTER 6: THE THIN LINE _____ 48

CHAPTER 7: PREACHER OF PERFORMER _____ 50

CHAPTER 8: WHEN GOD IS SILENT _____ 54

CHAPTER 9: FLAWED TRUTHS _____ 56

CHAPTER 10: THE SECRET REVEALED _____ 85

CHAPTER 11: THE POWER OF SILENCE _____ 93

CHAPTER 12: WHAT YOU DO DEFINES YOU _____ 102

CHAPTER 13: THE SECRET PLACE _____ 107

CHAPTER 14: GOD CAN RESTORE LOST TIME _____ 113

CHAPTER 15: UNLOCK YOUR LIMITATIONS _____ 118

CHAPTER 16: WHAT'S STOPPING YOU _____ 122

CHAPTER 17: FINDING GOD IN HIDDEN PLACES _____ 126

CHAPTER 18: LIVING FROM THE INSIDE OUT _____ 130

CHAPTER 19: TAKE ME TO THE KING _____ 134

CHAPTER 20: REVELATIONS FOR THE SOUL _____ 138

CHAPTER 21: THE NEXT CHAPTER _____ 144

FOREWORD

It is a delight to commend Bishop John C. Parks' latest book, Revelations for the Soul, as a milestone in advancing the Kingdom of God. It is an inducement for Pastors, Evangelists, Teachers, and all People of Christian Faith to pursue their call to "preach the word; be prepared in season and out of season; correct, rebuke and encourage with great patience and careful instruction [2 Timothy 4:2]."

Bishop John C. Parks is a living treasure among preachers who accept the yoke of

Pulpit Orator for the sake of Jesus Christ. He has been 'fighting the good fight' to advance the cause of the Kingdom for more than forty-seven (47) years – the better part of his lifetime. When it comes to preaching and teaching, Bishop Parks leads by example with this insight into successful preaching. Beyond that, though, he has lived life variously as a pastor and preacher, teacher, businessperson, and author.

Dr. Parks' choice of title recognizes the transforming power of the Word emanating from the pulpit. Only the gospel of Jesus Christ is powerful enough to transform hearts and lives and deliver us from the penalty and power of sin. One radical requirement from Jesus Himself is that "You must be born again" [John 3:7].

With this title, Bishop Parks continues his legacy of guiding us to the Peace of Christ, a value that resonates deeply with the Great Commission. This book, Revelations for the Soul, is a testament to that value, urging everyone to feel animated in their faith and play a dynamic part in spreading the gospel message. Your role in this mission is crucial and integral, and you are valued in this journey.

As we journey towards the goal of Christ's mission, we must remind ourselves of the urgency of sharing this book. It arrives at a crucial time, coinciding with the global celebration of the Feast of Pentecost—the Spiritual Birth of the Church of Jesus Christ. We, as the Church, Christ called to action. *"Veni, Sancte Spiritus!"* *"Veni, Sancte Spiritus!"* *"Veni, Sancte Spiritus!"* Come, Holy Spirit, and ignite the fire of your love in us. This urgency should motivate and instill a sense of commitment in the audience.

Honorable Philip Edward "Brave" Davis, Q.C., M.P.

Prime Minister of Commonwealth of the Bahamas

Leader of the Progressive Liberal Party (PLP)

THE AUTHOR'S PREFACE

"For when I preach the gospel, I cannot boast since I am compelled to preach. Woe to me if I do not preach the gospel **(I Corinthians 9:16)."**

The new performance vocabulary keeps me puzzled because it has become the standard terminology for the pop church's worship. Think about it. We used to have sanctuaries and pulpits; now, we have auditoriums, stages, and audiences. Some churches do not have a congregation; they have an audience. Many churchgoers expect the word "audience" to describe Sunday congregations. However, when you are in church service, you are not attending a play, a concert, or a movie. We (the church and the people who plan its worship) are not participating in entertaining Jesus in the hearers' hearts. Besides, if we are, it is merely not Christian praise. Yes, there is an element of style, character, and experience. However, the primary concentration of the preacher is to preach/teach the inerrant and infallible word of God! Our primary function is to reveal the mysteries and revelations in God's word. How can they hear without the preacher? [**Romans 10:14**].

Some pastors are great at everything except the pulpit. It takes work to prepare great messages week after week after week. Television ministries make it even harder, as people compare their pastors with superstar performers, televangelists, or megachurches. It is a lot to accomplish, and expectations are high. Some churches might just be looking for a break from that. The pastor is more than a preacher. The preacher matters. The pastor matters. The leader matters. In contrast, the preacher must have an element of performance and style to retain the congregation's attention. A church should never elevate performance above the unadulterated word of God and the responsibility for pastoral work. When we elevate performance, what you get from it —all across the congregation — might be an act.

Contemporary worship exacerbates this problem of performance versus the word of God. Some pastors only speak directly to all the unbelievers instead of including the believers who already know Jesus! Some churches forget about sending the members back into the world with a purpose. These churches' premise is, "Let's get the "world" in here and make Jesus therapeutic again." If non-believers, non-Christians, or skeptics are in your congregation, they will undoubtedly be; that is great. **Welcome them. Accept them. Invite them. Befriend them. Listen to their questions.** If they hear Christ's call on their lives and adopt the Christian faith as their own, it is a beautiful, incredible by-product of God's grace among us. However, the primary function of the Christian preacher is to reveal God through Jesus Christ. Preaching is not about the preacher. In **I Corinthians 9:16,** Paul says he cannot boast about anything. Unless God reveals His revelation and provides a Rhema word, the preacher is no more than a Sunday school teacher.

Teaching is not a microcosmic, disciplined, anticipatory remembrance of who we were, who we are, and who we are to be. Preaching is ALL about God through Jesus Christ. Preaching reaches the heart of the Christian to learn more about Jesus Christ. We come together and retell His story. The preached word of God strengthens us, and then we leave. When we go, the real work of ministry begins.

We, preachers and teachers, have the inerrant responsibility of providing revelation for the souls of our listeners. It is the revelation of the soul of man that makes us different. God created all living creatures with breath. However, he breathed into man, and he became a living soul. Consequently, the devil is not after our money, fame, or praise. The devil is after our soul. Therefore, we must have diligence and perseverance to avoid traps set by the latest fad or trend. Our mission is to provide revelations for the souls of all who hear us preach and teach the word of God from His inspired scriptures, the Bible.

As preachers and teachers, we stand as vessels of divine truth, delivering God's Word to those entrusted to our spiritual care. This responsibility is critical, for it carries eternal implications. Our role is not merely to impart information but to reveal the transformative power of God's Word in ways that penetrate the heart, challenge the mind, and awaken the soul.

Inerrancy in this responsibility means we must handle God's Word with precision, reverence, and integrity. The truths we teach are not our own; they are divinely inspired revelations intended to guide, convict, and comfort those who hear them. To deliver anything less than the fullness of God's revelation is to risk leading others astray and neglecting the very purpose of our calling.

This duty requires us to be diligent students of Scripture, seeking revelation before sharing it with others. We must approach the Word with humility, allowing the Holy Spirit to illuminate its meaning and application for our and listeners' lives. Through this process of divine illumination, we are equipped to provide spiritual nourishment to others.

Furthermore, this responsibility calls us to discern the specific needs of our listeners. Revelation is not a one-size-fits-all endeavor; it requires us to meet people where they are and address their struggles, doubts, and aspirations with the timeless truths of Scripture. Like the Apostle Paul, we must become "all things to all people" **[1 Corinthians 9:22]**, presenting the Gospel in ways that resonate with their unique circumstances without compromising its truth.

Finally, we must recognize the weight of accountability. James reminds us, "Not many of you should become teachers, my fellow believers because you know that we who teach will be judged more strictly" **[James 3:1].** This sobering reality should drive us to approach our ministry with fear and trembling, relying on God's grace to fulfill our calling faithfully.

Our role as preachers and teachers is to be conduits of divine revelation. God called us to illuminate the path of salvation, edify the body of Christ, and equip others to live lives that glorify God. This responsibility is both a privilege and a burden, but when carried out faithfully, it becomes a source of immense joy and eternal significance.

CHAPTER 1

THE WAKE-UP CALL

As Christians of the Gospel of Jesus Christ, we commit to His word and attempt to live life more abundantly. These thoughts ring true as people of all races, ethnicities, and lifestyles assemble for Sunday morning service each Sunday. These devout Christians seek to get a "Word" from the Lord. Many Sunday attendees receive a "Word" but leave without knowing God's purpose, plan, and promises. They go with excitement about the Sunday Church experience. However, they find it difficult to explain the Sunday experience to non-churchgoers or unbelievers. Many are content that they made it to church—others leave seeking more wisdom, knowledge, and understanding. These committed people leave church not feeling triumphant and prepare to press their way into a new week, trusting God. Unfortunately, these sincere people only receive a surface faith and fall short of the glory of God. George Ingram was one of them who felt a surface faith. He could quote many scriptures but did not grasp the scriptures' deeper meaning or revelation.

As was his custom, George Ingram sat in his sunroom early each Sunday morning. He adamantly took Sundays seriously as the Lord's Day and followed his scriptural understanding. Sundays were the Lord's Sabbath and were unique to him. He and Susan would awake early, drink their morning coffee, pray, and practice gratitude to their Heavenly Father for His goodness. Then, they would prepare themselves for their ritual of attending church. The church was more than a place to see their friends. The church was where they could praise God in the spirit of holiness.

Both George and Susan Ingram were successful in every area of their life. Like most Christians, they had occasional problems but no serious issues or crises. They achieved much success, and one could see their victory by the things they possessed and their successful three children. George did not have to boast of his success because people everywhere boasted of the favor of God in their lives. George would respond by saying God is good all the time, and all the time, God is good. He felt he had worked hard to do God's will, and his possessions reflected God's pleasure with his life and family. Unfortunately, George had lost his thirst for more knowledge about God. How could I have learned all I needed to know about God?" George thought. He loved his church, his pastor, and the church's ministry. However, all the sermons began to sound the same. He and Susan regularly studied the bible and received thoughts to enhance their life. They did not consider themselves Bible scholars, but they did possess biblical knowledge and biblical truths. Many people suggested to George that he had a ministerial calling. George appreciated those wonderful thoughts but knew God had not spoken to him.

George stared at himself in his bathroom mirror. "How did I plateau in my faith?" he said. He was more than a babe in Christ. "Have we plateaued, Susan?" He would often ask. What if there is more to the Bible than we are receiving? Can we comprehend God and His word in a 45-minute sermon and one-hour Bible Study?

After George and Susan finished their Sunday ritual, he felt that this Sunday was different. He stepped into his front yard and looked down his street. He attributed God's favor to his life as measured by his possession. On this particular Sunday, he had an epiphany. People around him who were atheists, unbelievers, and agnostics were successful, too. There was little noticeable difference between his lifestyle and most of them in his neighborhood. Before today, he did not notice the similarity. He proudly boasted of being a Christian and would witness to everyone he met. Now he realized that when he left home for his on-time arrival at the church, he saw most of the cars in his neighborhood still parked. The cars were still in their driveway when he, Susan, and their kids returned from dinner after church. George's confusion stemmed from how his neighbors had a similar lifestyle but did not attend church or Bible study.

Susan knew her husband so well. Once George was on to something, he was like a "bulldog." He was relentless in his determination to understand everything. His strength was also his weakness, as he never let anything go. He always had to get a clear resolution to all questions. George surveyed his accomplishments and realized non-churchgoers and unbelievers had the same possessions, and many had more. His confusion created a thirst for a deeper understanding of why there was no distinction. Our faith in God should translate into something more tangibly different. Do we genuinely understand the scriptures, or are we still babes in Christ after all these years in the church?

George walked into the kitchen to speak with Susan. "Sweetie, I am thoroughly confused by what's in my mind," George said. "Pastor Howell preached about *mountain-moving faith*, and our excitement about God made us rejoice." "But, Susan, when have we had to move a mountain?" Susan stood in amazement. In her mind, God granted them the perfect life – a great family, kids, great friends, great jobs, and an extraordinary life. "What brought these thoughts on George," Susan said. "We know God blessed us with so much. We cannot even count His blessings and love toward us." "Yes, that's correct, Susan, but have we ever moved a mountain,' George continued. We said amen and clapped our hands as Pastor Howell preached. But what was he talking about." George felt that he was experiencing an awakening. He did not quite understand why he had these thoughts. Perhaps the Holy Spirit led him into a deeper search and a greater thirst for God. One thing he was sure of was that his plateau in faith was unacceptable. He knew that God could not reside in clichés and surface faith. "What am I going to do to find the answer to my questions and confusion," George thought. Susan invited George into their prayer room. When confusion of any kind erupted, they would go to their prayer room for an answer. Their prayer room was their go-to place to seek God. They both valued prayer but wondered whether they prayed "surface prayers." Now, they would pray for Christ Jesus to take them beyond "surface faith" and into the deep things of God. After the prayer, George and Susan picked up their Bible and searched further. They realized that the Word of God provided answers to eradicate surface faith.

"Surface Faith is an outward showing of trust in God that only exists on the surface and does not genuinely dwell in the heart because of a lack of deep revelations of God's Word."

Jesus Christ often encountered and addressed surface faith throughout His time on earth. He taught about it and called it out when people practiced it before Him. Sometimes, religion can make us feel that God knows us and that we know Him. However, the Apostle Paul was adamant that we could have a zeal of God and not have knowledge of **God [Romans 10:2-4].** Incredibly, we can have a passion (great energy or enthusiasm) for a God we do not know. We see this phenomenon every day. People are passionate about many causes and fully commit to them – Black Lives Matter,

Civil Rights, Football Teams, etc. However, this passion does not suggest we know the leader or even understand the cause.

Quoting Isaiah 29:13, Jesus says,

"These people draw near to me with their mouths and honor me with their lips, but their hearts (emotions and feelings) are far from me. And in vain they worship Me teaching as doctrines the commandments of men,'" **[St. Matthew 15:8, 9].**

From these verses, we can see there was an outward profession of loving or trusting God and honoring Him with the words spoken, but the heart **(mind)** did not match. The result is vain worship, false teaching, or, best, surface faith. On the contrary, when the heart believes and the mouth confesses that God raised Lord Jesus from the dead, **Romans 10:9, 10** tells us the result is **saving faith.**

It is relatively simple. The heart cannot value or love what it does not know or understand. We can care for people. However, true love abides when we know them. This nature is not odd. We casually say we love people we do not know, and our expression of love does not match what our heart says about them. Such is the case with a God we cannot see. How can we love a God we cannot see? Our only option is to have a more profound revelation of His word. In other words, God is His Word.

Our only chance of truly knowing God is to receive revelations of His Word. Our surface faith introduces us and sustains us in the administration and operation of the church. Surface faith teaches us to have good behavior and do good things. However, surface faith leads to surface prayers, resulting in a surface understanding of God. We focus on attempting not to sin, but the more significant issue is surface faith. Christ covers our sins through redemption by His blood **[Ephesians 1:7-8].** God forgives our sins through confession **[I John 1:9-10].** However, surface faith makes us fall short of the glory of God **[Romans 3:23].**

George realized that his concern was legitimate. "Our regular visit to church does not make us know God," George said to Susan. Receiving revelations that change our hearts and minds from the inside out is how we develop a personal relationship with an omniscient, omnipresent, and omnipotent God through Christ Jesus, our Lord.

Reflection

Does your faith in Christ Jesus reside on the surface, or does it penetrate your heart and change you from the inside out? Doing good does not make us good. God wants us to do well, but He has more interest in our following after His righteousness **[St. Matthews 6:33].**

Where are you, and WHY? What must God do to make you want to go deeper with Him? To see that He has much more for you. There is so much more He wants to introduce you to, so much He wants to show you, so much He has in store for you – if only you will go deeper. He will even walk you out and talk you through it. We spend time and are passionate with everyone, and we do not comprehend the value of God's kingdom. We spend years getting an education to be proficient in our subject matter. However, we could only muster up enough knowledge within us to get us to surface faith.

God loves you SO much that He allows you to determine how deep you are willing to go with Him. He does not "demand it." He encourages us to go deeper: **"Taste and see that the Lord is good." [Psalm 34:8].**

The deep things of God are a dimension in the Kingdom where the revelations and heavenly wisdom are hidden. This dimension is not accessible to everyone.

The choice of how deep you are willing to go with Him rests on YOU. However, if you decide to dive below the surface with Him, he will show you the deep things of God! **[I Corinthians 2:10-11].** The deep things of God are in the spiritual realm. There are dimensions in the kingdom. The deep things of God are not accessible to everyone. It takes an intimacy with God to access this dimension, the hidden wisdom of God. Breathtakingly beautiful revelations that He will reveal to you as you dive deeper into intimacy with Him through His Word that will make you breathless! God desires you to go deeper into His kingdom.

When you choose to do so, He blesses you much more than you can imagine. You only have to keep digging deeper. Keep trusting… Keep believing… **St. Matthews 13:44** says we should treat God's kingdom as a treasure hidden in a field. God planted hidden and heavenly wisdom available to us and wants us to find this treasure.

"Again, the kingdom of heaven is like unto **treasure hid in a field**; when a man hath found, he hideth, and for joy thereof goeth and selleth all that he hath, and buyeth that field." **[St. Matthews 13:44]. That is how valuable the revelation of God becomes – we are willing to give all to obtain it.**

We must understand that God's word is a treasure hidden in a field and is not apparent to the eye. Surface faith will cause us to overlook the treasure. The requirement is looking for this treasure hidden in the Kingdom. When we find this treasure, we hide it. God expects us to hide this revelation in our hearts **[Psalms 119:11-16].** We cannot achieve this level of wisdom with surface faith. God will only provide this heavenly wisdom to those searching for it. The Apostle Paul was an ordinary man. What made Paul exceptional was searching for the hidden things of God. We will explore these precepts later in this book.

George and Susan left their prayer room excited. "We must schedule a meeting with Pastor Howell," George said. Yes, I am convinced there is more to this quest," Susan said. We must understand where the Spirit of Christ is leading us." George realized their plateau in faith was a jumping-off point to go deeper into God. They agreed not to miss this crucial moment in their lives.

George and Susan had a profound realization. They questioned the value of blessings when the Blessor is unknown. Often, we gauge our success and possessions by comparing them to others.

We mistakenly believe our commitment to the church and material wealth signifies a deep relationship with God. However, we overlook that God's love extends to everyone **[St. John 3:16]**. Yet, His treatment of each person is not uniform.

God gives grace to everyone.

One of the core tenets of the Christian faith is grace. The Apostle Paul extensively discussed grace, a topic many Christians focus on. However, they often overlook that God's grace is not exclusive to them but available to the entire world. This truth is evident in **St. John 3:16.**

"For God so loved the world that he gave his only begotten Son, that whosoever believeth in him should not perish, but have everlasting life."

We get so excited about "whosoever believeth in Him shall not perish; we ride quickly pass, "for God loves the world. This statement defines that god does not only love those who receive salvation. God loves the world. The Bible describes the world as those who oppose God.

God gave his only begotten son to die on the cross for the sins of humanity. The word begotten in Hebrew is *Yalad*, which means to bring forth. Therefore, we see that God did love the world and brought forth His Son to die for the sins of humanity. God, the Father, demonstrated His great love for His creation. When Saint John uses the word "world" in his Gospel, it generally refers to anyone who radically opposes God and His ways. John further instructs us that the world will hate us because the world hates Christ **[St. John 15:18]**. Nevertheless, it was precisely out of love for this same world that hates Him that God the Father sent His Son. "Susan, I have a greater understanding of why we have surface faith," said George." We tout our uniqueness in God's eyes because of God's grace. However, God's grace expands beyond our salvation. God's grace is His goodness. This goodness is available to everyone. George's epiphany helped him escape the belief that His blessings connected to the church. Now, he understood how the role of grace juxtaposed. Our blessings are not because of our membership in a church. Our blessings are because God loves His creation. When we accept **Romans 10:9,** God helps rescue us from the penalty of sin. George stepped back into his front yard and looked around his neighborhood. Now, he understood

God the Father demonstrated His great love He has for all of His creation. God so loved the world that He brought forth His Son to die on the Cross-for the sins of humanity.

Why his neighbors had possessions. The church and God's grace are mutually exclusive. If we attend church, we should have an excellent knowledge of God and receive the spiritual gifts of God. However, we cannot measure our spiritual gifts in material things. George suddenly became overwhelmed. This new understanding shook his faith. He measured his relationship with God based on his possessions and lifestyle. He never stopped to think that his neighbors do not attend church and have as much or more. God's grace extends beyond the four walls of a church.

Our salvation is by grace through faith **[Ephesians 2:8-9]**. Because his neighbors did not attend church, it did not mean that they did not have faith or knowledge of God. Surface faith is enough to get God's help but not enough to enter God's kingdom.

"Susan, please contact the Pastor's office and schedule a meeting with Pastor Howell as soon as possible," George asked. George's awakening caused him to thirst for a better understanding of God and His Kingdom. George realized that the zeal and enthusiasm of the church made him excited and feel good every Sunday. However, he was just a cut above the rest of the members of his community who did not attend church. He could boast about receiving Christ and his thirty years of membership at New Believers Baptist Church of Houston, Texas. He also gained a greater awareness of why many of his fellow Christians were struggling physically, emotionally, and spiritually. They, too, plateaued with surface faith.

Thursday evening came quickly. George and Susan entered Pastor Howell's office urgently. They had so many questions that required answering. Their awakening revealed that they only had surface faith. This was not enough. They wanted God's promises and an intimacy with God that went beyond the church.

"Pastor Howell, we received an awakening a few days ago that we urgently needed to discuss with you," George said. "We believe that we have not grown spiritually in our faith walk. Yes, we reaffirm and commit to the church's vision. We support your pastoral ministry and vision. However, we noticed that the people who do not commit to church are no different from us. Most are hardworking people attempting to succeed and earn the right to a quality life. How can we genuinely witness to others when our testimony differs from those out of the church?" George said. Pastor Howell leaned back in his chair. He was somewhat surprised about George's comment that there was no noticeable difference between his membership's benefits and the non-churchgoer's walk.

Pastor Howell responded with the traditional church response. "George, we walk by faith and not sight," Pastor Howell said. "You have to trust that God will keep all of His promises. God does not designate a certain time to perform these promises. It is a faith walk." George politely interrupted Pastor Howell. His concern was Pastor Howell's response, which was more "church talk" about the promises of God, walking by faith, trusting in the Lord, and getting to heaven. He knew there was more. George asked Pastor Howell, "What about the deep things of God?" "The Apostles were ordinary and unlearned men, but God inspired them with revelations and the mystery of the kingdom." Pastor Howell continued expressing his belief that we must study the Bible and let God speak to our hearts. He quoted the same scriptures that he and Susan had heard for twenty years at Belleview Church. Both George and Susan respectfully listen to Pastor Howell continue to give the surface response to a need for a deeper understanding.

George and Susan left Pastor Howell's office confused and agitated. Pastor Howell suggested to them that the characters in the Bible were heavenly chosen people of a particular lineage. Not everyone could achieve these revelations. God gives these unique and spiritual gifts to the special few and those God called into ministry. However, George realized that many preachers he faithfully listened to preach topologically. "Everyone keeps talking about things and possessions, but the Bible talks about spiritual gifts and the spiritual things of God," George said. **I Corinthians 12** lists all of these spiritual gifts. We don't see them in operation in our church or other churches in our community." How are we going to clear these questions up, George? Everyone is giving us the same answer. Judge your relationship with God by your God-given ability and possessions. Our church does not preach the more profound things of God." Susan responded. George became frustrated. He graduated from Bible College. His confusion was that he remembered that Pastor Howell had taught him to study to show himself approved by God. Consequently, he realized this knowledge could only come from deeper study. Therefore, George and Susan visited the Family Christian Bible store and purchased a Hebrew concordance, and a Hebrew Bible. We must commit the time to uncover this mystery through deep study," George and Susan agreed as she walked into the kitchen to prepare dinner.

Reflections.

Teacher or performer is the real question. Our efforts to appease the masses often result in surface teaching, yielding to surface faith. The congregation dictates what they like based on their response to the spoken word. Consequently, they condition the teacher to provide them with a word that has entertainment value. The teacher must remember their assignment. This assignment requires both preaching in season and out of season [2 Timothy 4:2]. Otherwise, the only value the church will provide is the scratching of "itchy" ears and fall short of the glory of God.

While George left frustrated with his meeting with Pastor Howell, his soul was not free. He realized that he, too, had become comfortable with his surface faith. The testing of his faith was not complete. His prosperity as a middle-class professional resolved most of his challenges in life. He understood now that his prosperity would not deter the plans and scheme of the devil and his demonic forces. Spiritual attacks are actual. He sat it took to heart **St. John 10:10**, "The devil comes to steal, kill, and destroy. In addition, George thought he could never give his best to his Creator unless he fully understood the Word of God. God intends for us to grow in grace and the knowledge of our Lord and Savior, Jesus Christ **[2 Peter 3:18]**.

George walked into the kitchen, where he found Susan feverishly working to prepare their dinner. She was so excited that she was preparing his favorite meal – lamb chops with green jelly, asparagus, and little red potatoes. His favorite dessert was key lime pie. George walked up behind Susan and gave her a big hug. "I am so happy you are joining me on this journey of discovery," George said. Susan responded, "As usual, we have arrived at the same junction. There must be more." They gave each other a "fist bump" to express their planned teamwork.

George's best friend was Richard Shaw. They grew up together, played high school sports, and lived in the same neighborhood. "I have to call Richard and tell him of our discovery and awakening honey," George said. "I would not want to leave him out of this new journey. He might be busy, but I should ask him and Cathy Shaw about their interest," George said. "That is a great idea. We can study together," Susan responded. George called Richard and explained everything to him. Richard and Cathy agreed to visit their George and Cathy's home on Thursday evening. They had also arrived at a point where they felt stagnated. Church sounded like a repeat of last year. The sermons merged. There are sixty-six books in the Bible, but most heard about the four Gospels and occasionally Paul's letter to churches. They seldom went into the Old Testament, but it was mostly Genesis and Exodus when they did. They were happy with their church, the pastor, and the ministry. However, they lacked a deeper walk with God. Why did they still have a thirst after 30 years of seeking God's will?

Thursday came quickly, and Richard and Cathy showed up promptly, as always. They feasted and enjoyed the beautiful meal prepared by Susan. Then, they all went into the family room to discuss George's new desire to go deeper into God. George realized that he did not have the necessary knowledge. George and Susan wanted to get Shaw's opinion on his concern. He did not want to become legalistic and place God in a self-design Box.

George Took about an hour to explain meticulously his new thoughts to Richard and Cathy. Richard said, "Wow, I never thought about scripture that way, George. We thought trust was trusting in the preached word only. We felt the Holy Spirit gave the rest to us. "That's how we miss the mark, Richard," George responded. Sometimes, what we consider the Holy Spirit speaking to us is our carnal desires. Because we are religious, we present our thoughts under a spiritual pretense. Otherwise, people would consider us a heretic. No one can truly argue with us when we say, the Lord or the Holy Spirit told me."

George went a little deeper. "Because we see God speaking to Moses and the Old Testament Prophets, we use this same approach to ourselves. We elevate ourselves to that ministry level without realizing that we are not Moses or any Biblical Patriarchs whose name is in the Hall of Faith. These patriarchs were leading nations or speaking to an entire race of people. We relegate God to lead us to speak to one person. It is presumptuous of us to minimize the Bible and assign a role to the Holy Spirit that the scripture does not instruct on." Richard responded I see how we have missed the mark.

We compare ourselves to those genuinely committed to our example. We misinterpret the word of prophecy as Prophet and misquote Joel. "Susan said, "I have people telling me what the Lord said for them to tell me, but they constantly have problems, conflicts, and bad decisions. If the Holy Spirit was speaking, why does their fruit say otherwise?" You are right, "said Cathy. The Bible is God's Word. He gave us the Bible to know Him, Preachers to speak about Him, and the Holy Spirit to remind us about Him and help us worship Him in Spirit and Truth.

"Count us in," said Richard and Cathy. Now, the journey begins. George said that God's primary concern is our soul.

Richard expanded on George's thought by emphasizing that the condition of the soul determines the trajectory of our lives, both now and in eternity. He explained that a soul aligned with God is a source of peace, joy, and purpose, while a soul estranged from God experiences unrest and spiritual death. Richard underscored that God's concern for our souls is evident in the sacrifice of Jesus Christ, who bore the weight of humanity's sin to redeem our souls. For Richard, this act of divine love reveals that the soul's restoration and salvation are central to God's mission.

Together, George and Richard agreed that God's focus on the soul stems from its ability to reflect His image and glorify Him. They discussed how God's concern is not merely to save us from eternal separation but to nurture and transform our souls into vessels of His love and grace. This transformation allows believers to impact the world for His kingdom while preparing for their eternal home. Their shared conviction is that the soul's eternal significance demands our attention and devotion, aligning our priorities with God's and allowing Him to shape us into His likeness.

"Susan, is it possible we worship God with a **"surface faith,"** George asked. We hear the Word of God. We study the Word of God, and we put in practice the Word of God, but do we truly understand what we are hearing?" Susan stood in unbelief at her husband. They devoted most of their lives following the precepts and doctrine of their church. Their devotion to god was 30 years deep and now George goes off on a tangent. "George, can't you see what the Lord has done for us!" "Yes, baby! However, everyone on this block of twenty-five homes have as much or more. Only five other families devote themselves to George and Susan's attempt to worship and witness to their community.

Susan paused thoughtfully before answering. "Yes, it's entirely possible to worship God with a 'surface faith,' and honestly, many of us may fall into it without even realizing it. Surface faith is when our relationship with God is more about outward appearances or routine practices than a deep, transformative connection with Him. It is when we go to church, sing the songs, and even say the right prayers, but our hearts and minds are not truly engaged with God. It is a faith that touches the lips but has not reached the depths of the soul. Jesus warned about this when He quoted Isaiah, saying, 'These people honor me with their lips, but their hearts are far from me.' Surface faith looks alive on the outside, but it lacks the roots needed to sustain real growth and intimacy with God."

She continued, "Surface faith often arises when we prioritize tradition or convenience over a genuine pursuit of God. It is easier to check spiritual boxes—reading a verse of the day or attending church—than to wrestle with God in prayer or let His Word challenge and change us. However, true worship, the kind that pleases God, requires more than a superficial approach.

CHAPTER 2

GOD'S PRIMARY CONCERN OUR SOUL

We focus on this, so we must put much energy into ensuring our health is in check and our minds function based on the knowledge gained through education or experience. We invest significant money to ensure our minds stay at peak performance; however, the critical component of our triune needs to be prioritized. When Abba Father created man, He performed a unique act as found in **Genesis 2:7. Genesis 2:7** says, "And the LORD God formed man *of* the dust of the ground, and breathed into his nostrils the breath of life, and man became a living soul. No other creature in God's creation possesses a soul. **God made things (rock, dirt, etc.), living things (Things that fly and in the ocean), living creatures (things that walk on the ground), and man who operates a living soul.** God programmed every other creature with instincts and survival skills. However, man has a soul.

God breathes life into the nostrils of man. He gave man the breath of life. The "breath of life" **Hebrew word, *nesema,"*** God's breath gave Adam life, spiritual understanding **[Job 32:8],** and a functioning conscience **[Proverbs 20:27].** Adam's life came from God's breath. Adam's uniqueness existed because God made him in His image. God's breath may be a synonym for His word **[Psalms 33:6].** Man, therefore, is a combination of dust and divinity. **Man became a living soul**, or a living man, capable of performing animal life functions, eating, drinking, walking, etc., but of thinking, reasoning, and discoursing as a rational creature. God fearfully and wonderfully made us **[Psalms 139:14].** Elihu refers to this creation history by saying, "I also am formed out of the clay **[Job 33:4- 6].** The breath of the Almighty hath given me life **[Job 33:6].**"

There is a spirit in man. However, only God's most incredible creation has a soul. When a man dies, his body returns to the dust, and his spirit or breath ceases. However, his soul returns to God to live in eternity with Him, or man's soul joins the devil and his demons in the lake of fire for eternity in torment.

Reflections.

We spend many wakening hours attempting to develop the mind without understanding that God does not speak to our mind. The Holy Spirit only bears witness to the spirit of man **[Romans 8:16].** Therefore, God by His Holy Spirit speaks to man's soul or his spirit. If the spirit of man does not recognize the voice of God through the Word of God, he cannot comprehend spiritual things **[I Corinthians 2:14].**

The LORD God, *El Shaddai,* formed man. Of the other creatures, God *created* and *made,* but God uniquely formed man. Which denotes attention with great accuracy and exactness? God's workmanship exceeded the dust from whence we came. Our bodies are living sacrifices to God

13

[Romans 12:1], as living temples [I Corinthians 6:19], then these bodies after death shall shortly be new-formed like Christ's glorious body [Philippians 3:21]. However, our uniqueness is not the accuracy and exactness of our human body.

Let the soul, God has breathed into us, breathe after Him, and let it be for Him since

It is From Him.

We are in His image and likeness, and not of ourselves.

God gave us a soul. God created our soul from His breath [Ecclesiastes 12:7]. Therefore, God is not only the Creator but also the Father of spirits. Let the soul, which God breathed into us, breathe after Him, and let it be for Him since it is from Him. Into His hands, let us commit our spirit to Him. The body is a worthless, useless, loathsome pile of clay dust if the soul does not animate it. To God, who gave us these souls, we must shortly give an account of our souls. We spend much time gaining possessions. However, Jesus admonishes that we can gain the whole world and lose our soul [St. Mark 8:36].

Jesus asks, "What profits a man to gain the whole world and lose his soul," referring to his eternal life [Matthew 16:26]. The Old and New Testaments reiterate that we are to love God completely, with the whole "soul," which refers to everything in us that makes us alive [Deuteronomy 6:4-5; Mark 12:30]. Whenever the word "soul" is used, it can refer to the whole person, whether physically alive or in the afterlife.

The word "spirit" denotes something different in scripture, although Hebrew and Greek words translated as "spirit" also have the concept of breath or wind at their roots. We understand the difference by looking at the context of the verses that refer to the spirit of man. Unlike the soul, which is alive both physically and eternally, the spirit can be either alive, as in the case of believers, [1 Peter 3:18], or dead, as unbelievers are [Colossians 2:13, Ephesians 2:4-5]. The spiritual part of a believer in Jesus Christ is that which responds to the things that come from the Spirit of God, understanding and discerning them spiritually. The spiritually dead perceive the things of the Spirit to be "foolishness" because, in his spiritually dead conditions, he cannot determine the things of the Spirit [1 Corinthians 2:12-14]. The spirit is that part of us that God enables us to know and worship Him, the part of humanity that "connects" with God, who Himself is Spirit [St John 4:24]. While the two words, spirit, and soul, are often interchangeable, the primary distinction between soul and spirit in man is that the spirit is the animate life or the seat of the senses, desires, affections, and appetites. The soul is that part of us that connects to God or refuses to connect. Our souls relate to His Spirit, either accepting His promptings and conviction, thereby proving that we belong to Him [Romans 8:16], or resisting Him and proving that we do not have spiritual life [Acts 7:51].

Since God wanted man to have a soul, let us not be of those foolish people who despise their own souls by preferring their bodies before them [Proverbs 15:32]. When our Lord Jesus breathed on his disciples, saying, "Receive you the Holy Ghost." He was He that first breathed into man's nostrils the breath of life. He who made the soul alone is able to make it new. Our soul is essential to God. Our soul is God's priority. Our body and our mind go to the grave [Ecclesiastes 9:10].

The soul returns to God. God is a spirit [St. John 4:24], and He speaks first to your soul, and then your soul translates it to your mind as a thought. God can only talk to us. Soul because it is His spirit in us. The spirit of the man is different from the Holy Spirit. The Holy Spirit of God speaks

14

to the soul of man. God's concern is your soul [I Thessalonians 5:23]. Over and very over again in scripture, the Bible refers to us as "souls" Exodus [Exodus 31: 14, Proverbs 11:30]. The human soul is part of decay, which is eternal – which part lives after the body dies. Jesus said, "We are not to fear men, who can only kill the body, but not the soul [St. Matthews 10:28]. The human spirit and soul are different [Hebrews 4:12]. Jesus Christ, because He was fully man and God, also had a soul. His soul experienced anguish at Gethsemane while he prayed before going to the cross. He said, "My soul is very sorrowful, even to death [St. Matthews 26:36-46]." Psalms also speaks of the soul of the Messiah, saying that His soul will not be abandoned to Sheol nor His body to corruption or decay [Psalms 16:9-10, Acts 13:35-37].

The human soul is imperishable; every human soul will be somewhere for eternity [Daniel 12:2; Matthew 25:46]. This is a sobering thought—every person you have ever met is a soul living in a body, and that soul will last forever. Some will reject the love of God, and as a result, they will have to pay for their sins with death [Romans 6:23], and since the soul is eternal, Eternal death is their end. Those who accept the free gift of forgiveness and Christ's atoning sacrifice will experience the opposite—eternal life and peace in heaven with God [Psalm 23:2].

We focus on our mind, body, and spirit. However, we overlook the fourth part of man. The fourth part is under the radar of our minds. We seek knowledge for the mind. We seek health and fulfillment for our bodies. We strive to preserve our lives and live long. However, the church falls short of giving us knowledge about our souls. Consequently, we cannot discover the deep things of God. Much of what we gain from listening or reading the word of God is knowledge. Knowledge is for the natural mind, which cannot perceive or receive the spiritual and deep things of God.

What is the difference between the soul and the spirit?

We can find the words "soul" and "spirit" throughout the Bible, each occurring hundreds of times in the Old and New Testaments. The Hebrew word for "soul" is *nephesh*. Nephesh is one's true self or character. What does that tell us? We get the sense that *Nephesh* speaks of the very essence of a person. This **understanding** comes into focus when we examine **Deuteronomy 6:5**, the first and chief commandment given to the children of Israel:

Deuteronomy 6:5
"And thou shalt love the Lord thy God with all thine heart, <u>soul,</u> and all thy might."

This scripture clearly defines God's interest in our souls and distinguishes between our hearts and souls. **St Luke 10:17** says, "He answered,' Love the Lord your God with all your heart and soul and with all your strength and your entire mind.' The heart and mind are different from the soul.

Some theologians and religious pundits say NO. They say the living soul is the body. However, God gave living creatures a body but not a soul. *Yah-ah [God's name]* removes the spirit of men, so we have to die. However, the soul returns to Him. **Immortality is the indefinite continuation of a person's existence, even after death**. To understand this question fully, we must realize Yah's creation. He created and made:

15

- Things – He spoke into existence [**Genesis 1:3-10, 1419**].
- Living things – He spoke into existence [**Genesis 1;11-13, 28**] – need water
- Living creatures – He created into existence [**Genesis 1; 20-25**] – need water, food, and spirit.
- Living beings. He formed man in His image and likeness [**Genesis 1:26-28 and Genesis 2:7**] – need water, food, spirit, and soul.

He made likeness and us in His image (temunah, species or capabilities) [Demuth, Character] so we could become like Christ Jesus, Sons of God. However, Adam's fall changed it all. Man has four components instead of three (**Tri-part**).

- A BODY like every living creature [**Genesis 2:7**]
- A MIND and SPIRIT, likeness Abba Father [**Genesis 1:26, 27**]
- A SOUL [**Genesis 2:7**], immortality.

PURPOSE FOR THE FOUR PARTS.

BODY – God created a physical body for living things, creatures, and living beings to reproduce in the physical world [**Genesis 1:21, 22 -28**]. God made Angels as beings but do not have bodies, so they cannot reproduce or birth other angels.

MIND – God created our minds to retain our various abilities [logic, skill, memory, etc., and five senses [seeing, hearing, tasting, smelling, touching, and emotions]. Now, some people are looking for God in their minds. They think, "If I could only figure things out, then I could find God." The mind cannot discern spiritual things [**I Corinthians 2:14**].

SPIRIT – "little" s" - God gave us a spirit to contact, experience, and worship Him [**St. John 4:22-24**]. God breathes into us His breath of life (human spirit) [**Genesis 2:7**]. The human spirit is man's spirit, God's breath [**Job 32:8, Job 27:3**]. The Holy Spirit speaks to our spirit [**Romans 8:16-17**]

SOUL. - God made us a living soul [**Genesis 2:7**]. **The word "Soul in Hebrew is *nephesh* and means your unique self. God gave man character so man could develop Godly character".** His desire is for us to be like Christ [**Romans 8:29**]. To develop our character is what God is after, to experience the great things of Abba Father and impact others [**Isaiah 38:15-18**] – we seek to create our mind, body, and spirit, but many do not work on the health of our soul [**Mark 8:34-38**]. Abba Father wants our soul (character) to prosper [**3 John 1:2**]. The LORD is good [**fit the purpose**] unto them that wait [*Qavah* – Hebrew= connected to Him like a three-stranded cord] for him, to the soul that seeks Him [**Lamentation 3:25**].

The devil is not after your body; it is dust. He is not after your mind; your mind is already filthy; he cannot take your human spirit; it is the breath of God. However, Satan is after our soul [character]. It is our character that people see, experience, benefit, or destroy. Bad character will hinder even our parents or family from having anything to do with us. We become deplorable in the world and useless in the Kingdom of God. Abba Father has a soul [**Isaiah 42:1-9**]. The Bible provides instructions on glorifying God by building character [I.e., Abraham, Moses, David, Paul, Peter, etc.]. God rewards us based on our character **[Job 10:1-2]**.

The devil understands the soul, which is why Satan works to wound our soul **[Job 2:3-3-5]**. The human soul is that part of a man or woman that is not physical. The soul is the "true self"—who a person is [CHARACTER]. The soul is the center of our unique self and identity. Man cannot kill the soul; it returns to God **Matthews 10:28]**. The Apostle John sees "under the altar the souls of those who had been slain because of the word of God and their testimony they had maintained **[Revelation 6:9]**. All souls are immortal **[St. John 11:26],** but they are not eternal in the same way that God is. God is the only infinite being in that He alone is without a beginning or end. God has always existed and will always continue to exist. Scriptures instruct us, *"You shall love the Lord your God with all your heart, soul (nephesh), and all you might."* The New Testament reiterates this commandment: *Love the Lord your God with every passion of your heart, with all the energy of your being, and with every thought within you.* **[Matthew 23:27].** This type of love takes over everything! It is a love expressed with "the whole of the affections of the heart, with great fervency and ardor of spirit, in the sincerity of the soul, and with all the strength of grace a man has, with such love that is as strong as death."

Nephesh that brings revelation.

In Psalm 19, David wrote, ***"How the sky reveals God's glory... no speech or words are used, no sound is heard, yet their message goes out to the entire world and is heard to the ends of the earth".*** Have you ever considered that, just like the sky, your life should send this same message to the world? Your life—your words and actions—should reveal God to the people around you! This means we should love God with all our life and for all our life. In addition, when we do – when we love God with all of who we are and with everything – we <u>bear witness</u> to others! It means to love Him in everything we do, every word we speak, and every minute of every day.

We must feed the soul.

What we feed will live, and what we starve will die. We feed our bodies and our minds. However, we do not nourish our souls. The human body has a remarkable ability to assimilate all manner of foods. No matter the variety of a person's taste, the body digests the foods. The body survives on various foods or will exist for periods on one meal. Scientists call bread **"the staff of life"** because it contains almost all the nutrition needed for the human body. Jesus talked about the "Bread of Life," I want us to focus on this bread.

Everyone knows bread. Everyone eats bread today. Many people have baked bread. We know about bread. There are several apparent contrasts between heavenly bread and earthly bread. You may think of others, but let me examine a few differences.

1) Earthly bread is artificial; heavenly bread is God-made.

.2) we eat earthly bread regularly; we consume heavenly bread only once.

3) Earthly bread has many earthly ingredients; heavenly bread has one heavenly component.

4) We bake earthly bread in man's oven; God prepares heavenly bread.

The children of Israel should have understood more about heavenly bread. Instead, they said the bread was manna. Manna means, "What is this?" They knew their ancestors and received daily portions of manna from heaven. Jesus referred to this manna in the New Testament. However, the Bread of Life is the Bread of Heaven **[St. John 6:32]**.

Manna came down, and the Bread of Life came down - how? How did the bread of life come down from heaven? Luke, the physician, tells us, ". The Holy Spirit shall come upon thee, and the power of the Highest shall overshadow thee," The virgin birth assured the bread of life to be heavenly bread.

We should take opportunities to talk to people about salvation. We can ask, "How does a person go to heaven?" The answer given will tell you if their view of the Bread of Life is earthly or heavenly. Earthly Bread says, "Be baptized, join the church, do good works, make reforms, etc." Heavenly bread states, "...believe in the Lord Jesus Christ, and thou shall be saved and be reconciled with God **[2 Corinthians 5:18-21]. The Bread of Life is holy**.

We must feed our souls with heavenly bread. This heavenly bread is the Word of God. The Bible never instructs us to read the word of God, but rather to show thyself approved. People study to obtain licenses, degrees, and diplomas. They are relentless in passing the test to reap their labor's benefits. However, these same people give casual concern to the Word of God. They read the Word and receive a philosophical thought. They consider their thought as accurate when someone else has the same idea. They take the scripture text as truth without understanding it, falling short of the revelation from the context. In hermeneutics, we obtain a revelation by reading the pre-text and post-text. The pre-text and post-text give us the context. The context is what God is saying to us. The context speaks volumes to our soul in what is lacking. We dig deeper into a profound understanding of God's word when we receive this revelation. This profound and deep understanding we call "revelation." The soul needs more than a "Word." The soul needs a revelation!

One of the most misinterpreted scriptures in the Bible is **St. Luke 6:38**. Many people use this scripture to speak about receiving money from God. They allege that if we sow (give money) into a ministry, considered "good" ground, men shall bring into our bosom good measure, press down, shaken together, and run over. People who do not study or receive the revelation of the scripture foolishly begin sowing money, expecting to receive money. We do not feed our souls because of the lack of revelation. Then, they leave with less in their wallet or purse, expecting God to supply money. When we do not feed our souls, our character remains unchanged.

Let us examine **St. Luke 6:38** to receive the "intended" revelation so our soul can receive and change our character. Remember, to receive a revelation, we must read the text, the pretext, and the post-text. Here we go,

THE TEXT

St. Luke 6:38 says, "Give, and it shall be given to you, good measure, press down, shaken together and running over shall give unto your bosom."

THE CONTEXT

What an amazing revelation! **St. Luke 6:38** is not about money. The revelation for the soul is simple. We must give love and mercy to others so that our heavenly Father can give love and mercy. If we demonstrate this character, our heavenly Father will motivate men to bring love and compassion into our bosom, pressed down, shaken together and running over. Now that the Word of God feeds our souls, we can see the change necessary to receive the perfect favor of God. Without this revelation, our current character will not change and we fall short of God's glory. We press our way and stunt our spiritual maturity.

Reflections.

We obtain a revelation by understanding the context of a scripture. The pre-text and post-text give us the context. The context is what God is saying to us. The context speaks volumes to our soul in what is lacking. We dig deeper into a profound understanding of God's word when we receive this disclosure. This profound understanding is "revelation." The soul needs more than a Word." The soul needs a revelation!

Satan attacks our souls.

Satan has no interest in anything three-dimensional. Three-dimensional is anything that our five senses can perceive. Satan's purpose and intent in taking from Job his precious possession was to harm Job's soul. His strategy was for Job to demonstrate a different character than in **Job 1 1-3.** Satan asked the question, what shall a man give in exchange for his soul **[St. Matthews 16:26].**" Let us examine this revelation closely by reviewing the context.

For what is a man profited ... - To gain the whole world means to possess it as our own - all its riches, honors, and pleasures.

"To lose his soul," means for God to cast away, shut out from heaven, and sends to hell. Christ implies two things in these questions:

1. That they who are striving to gain the world and are unwilling to give it up for the sake of religion will lose their souls; and,
2. If the soul is lost, the soul loses the chance for salvation. There is no redemption in hell.

People often judge natural things far more correctly than spiritual things; they are watchful concerning natural objects. They feel a deep interest in them, and they watch for every sign that may affect their interest. They quickly judge falsely. However, they feel no such interest in religious things. Hence, it happens that people who have good sense and much wisdom regarding worldly concerns often act foolishly regarding religion. They believe in reports respecting religion, revivals, and missions, which they despise on any other subject. They read and believe newspapers and other publications, which they would hold in contempt on any other topic but faith. They give a degree of weight to arguments against the Bible and against the doctrines of the gospel, to which they would attach little or no importance on any other subject. They sustain themselves in infidelity by arguments they would regard as of no force if the same kind of reasoning urged in defense of anything else. We must remember that Satan attacks our soul.

It is essential to watch the signs of the times [**Matthew 16:3**]. In the days of Christ, it was the duty of the Pharisees and religious leaders to look at the evidence that Jesus was the Messiah. The proofs were clear that He was the Messiah. It is also essential to look at the signs of the times in which we live. They are clear also. Much is going on by those who would diffuse the Bible. We should watch these signs to rejoice, pray with more fervor, and do our part to advance the kingdom of God. Little children should grow up believing they live in a critical age, enjoy many unique privileges, and must do much to spread the gospel to everyone we can. Even in childhood, they should pray and give to benefit others; most of all, they should give themselves to Christ to benefit others with the right spirit.

We should address unbelievers with deep feeling and faithfulness [**Mark 8:12**]. Jesus sighed deeply. So should we. We should not be harsh, sour, cold, and unfeeling when we address our fellow men about eternity. We should weep over them, pray for them, and speak to them, not as if we were better than they were, but with an earnest desire for their salvation. [**Acts 20:31, Philippians 3:18**].

People easily mistake plain instruction, **Matthew 16:7,** especially in cases where there is any chance of giving a worldly turn to the instruction. If people's thoughts - even those of Christians were more off from the world, and they thought less of the supply of their temporal wants, they would understand the truths of God's kingdom much better than they do. No man can understand the doctrines of religion aright whose principal concern is what he shall eat, drink, and wear. Hence, even Christians are often strangely ignorant of God's plainest truths. Thus, it is important to teach those truths to people before the world engross their thoughts.

We should not have undue anxiety about the supply of our wants. Christ supplied thousands in a desert by a word, and He can quickly provide for us [**Matthew 16:9-12**]. From His past goodness, we should learn to trust him for the future [**Matthew 16:9-12**]. We should be on our guard against error [**Matthew 16:11**]. Error is sly, artful, plausible, working secretly but effectually. We should always be cautious of what we believe and examine it by the word of God. False doctrines are often made as much like the truth as possible for the very purpose of deceiving. "Satan transforms himself into an angel of light" [**2 Corinthians 11:14**]. It is essential to ascertain our views of Christ [**Matthew 16:13-15**]. Our future destiny depends on this. We cannot be safe if we do not think and feel right respecting him. We should often, then, ask ourselves - we should ask one another - what we think of Christ.

The church is safe.

God only reveals to world the correct views of Christ [**Matthew 16:17**]. He does this by His word and Spirit. We should, then, search the Bible and pray that God would reveal His Son to us and enable us to confess Him boldly before people. George's revelation of the Holy Spirit's role in revealing Christ was a profound moment of clarity and transformation. As he meditated on Scripture, he realized that the Holy Spirit is not merely a helper or comforter but the divine agent who illuminates the truth of Christ to the human heart. George saw how the Spirit unveils the beauty and glory of Jesus, making His love, sacrifice, and victory real and personal. This revelation deepened George's gratitude and dependence on the Spirit, igniting a passion to live a life that reflected Christ's image through the Spirit's empowering presence.

The church is safe. It may be small, feeble, weep much, much opposed and ridiculed, mighty enemies, and the rich and the great may set themselves against it, but it is safe.

The church is safe, Matthew 16:18. It may be small, feeble, weep much, much opposed and ridiculed, mighty enemies, and the rich and the great may set themselves against it, but it is safe. Christ founded the church upon a rock. Its enemies shall never be able to overcome it. Jesus has promised it, and in all ages, He has shown that He remembered it. The church's enemies persecuted, opposed, ridiculed, and almost driven the church from the world, but there remains those who loved the Lord. The church shines forth "fair as the sun, clear as the moon, and most powerful army with banners.

Therefore, the church still exists. Feeble churches may mourn much iniquity may abound - the few pious people may weep in secret places, but Jesus hears every groans and counts every tear, so the church is safe. She is our friend, and not all the powers of hell shall prevail against His church.

We must exercise prudence in delivering truth, **Matthew 16:21**. We must tell the truth - when people prepare to receive it. This is true of young converts. They need milk and not strong meat. We must understand that the doctrines of the Bible are mysterious to them, but they will fully comprehend them as they grown in grace and the knowledge of Christ.

Peter, a young convert, did not understand the plain doctrine that Jesus must die for sin, yet he saw him later, and, most cordially, he loved it. It is evil and improper to attempt to counsel God or to think that we understand things better than He does [**Matthew 16:22-23**]. God's plan is the best, and though it does not fall within our views of "wisdom," we should be still. We do not know what He does now, yet we shall know hereafter.

We see what faith requires [**Matthew 16:24**]. We must deny ourselves. We must submit to trials. We must do our duty. We must welcome persecution [**Matthew 5:10**]. We must be, in all places, among all people, and in every situation. We must remain steadfast no matter what may happen. Come poverty, disease, persecution, death, it is ours to take up the cross and do our duty.

How foolish are some of the people of this world! [**Matthew 16:26**]. How worthless will all their wealth be? Anxiety, toil, and tears gain it. It never satisfies. It harasses them with constant care. Our possessions reduce no stress, alleviate no pain when sick, save no friend from death, give no consolation regarding the future, and may leave at any moment. Others will soon possess, and perhaps scatter in dissipation, what they have obtained by so much toil [**Psalms 39:6**]. Moreover, while they scatter or enjoy it, where shall the soul of him be who spent all his probation to obtain it? Alas! Lost, lost, lost - forever lost! Moreover, no wealth, man, devil, or angel can redeem him or give for his soul. The harvest will be past, the summer will end, and he will only receive salvation. In gaining the world, he made two things confident - disappointment and trouble here and an eternity of woe hereafter. How foolish and wicked is man!

The righteous should rejoice that Jesus came to our world. He will reward them [**Matthew 16:27**]. He will come as their friend, and they shall ascend with him to glory. The wicked should weep and wail that Jesus will come again to our world. He will punish them for their crimes [**Matthew 16:27**]. They cannot escape [**Revelation 1:7**]. Christ can come at any moment [**Matthew 16:28**]. We shall see Him as He is. When death comes, we must stand before him and give an account of the deeds done in the body. Satan's strategy is to usurp the glory and authority of God by motivating us to disobedience. When we are willfully disobedient, we corrupt our souls. We gain the things of the world, but we lose our souls and character. The LORD builds our soul by taking us from faith to faith [**Romans 1:17**]. He reveals the righteousness of God on this journey. This righteousness is one of the benefits of Christ's church.

Despite what some televangelists and pastors teach, there is no process. A process suggests that there is a beginning and an ending. We are on a journey. This journey is God's wisdom and intention to transform us into the image of Christ [**2 Corinthians 3:18**]. This transformation births us and grows us to become Sons of God. Satan knows God cannot speak to flesh, nor can flesh glorify Him. Only our soul or our character can glorify God. When we do well, it makes God look good. When we look bad, God seems helpless. Satan's ultimate desire is for God to look bad. Satan's every attempt to make God look bad through us is evident from Genesis through the book of Acts. Paul's, Peter's, and Jude's letters highlight our struggle with our adversary. His mission is subtle but deadly. We can allow religion to make us religious. Beneath our religion can lie evil intention. We compare ourselves and feel better about ourselves. We have the same attitude as the Pharisees who condemned the publican. However, Christ exalted the publican because of his open confession of guilt and sin. Consequently, Christ exalted the publican and condemned the Pharisee [**Luke 18:9-14**].

What does it prosper a man to gain the whole world and lose His soul? The perpetual errors coming from many religious leaders damage our souls. When we accept false doctrine, we feed our souls with error. Consequently, we should improve many things in our character. Because we see ourselves as religious, we believe we are acceptable to God. However, God did not create religion. Artificial religion attempts to explain God and develop a form of worship. We undervalue what God expects. God expects and demands more than worship. He demands spirit and truth. **John 4:23-24** records Jesus saying, "But the hour is coming, and is now here when the true worshipers will worship the Father in spirit and truth, for the Father is seeking such people to worship him. God is spirit, and those who worship him must worship in spirit and truth." What did He mean?

First, it is essential to understand what worship is. Many equate worship with singing and music in church. This is one aspect of prayer [**Psalm 100:2**], but worship is not limited to song. Worship is a full-life response to the object of our service. When we genuinely worship something, it affects the way we live. One way to look at worship is to consider it "worthwhile." When we worship something, we declare it worthy [**Psalm 145:3**]. The Greek word used for "worship" implies an attitude of reverence. It also includes such physical gestures as kissing the hand or kneeling [**Psalm 95:6**]. We worship something when we act as if it has value. By nature, human beings are worshippers. Sometimes, we focus our worship on that worthy of reverence (like God). Other times, it is misdirected (for instance, we worship our work, our bank accounts, fashion, or a political icon).

Worship is a life response to the worthiness of its object. When we worship God, we do so in response to who He is **[Psalm 52:9]**. Our attitudes and actions reflect that we believe God's character and conduct are worthy of praise and adoration. Sometimes, we attempt to worship through corporate singing, teaching, and giving. We also expressed worship daily through prayer, Scripture reading, acts of kindness, gratitude, pure thoughts, and the like. Next, we must examine what it means to worship in spirit and truth. It is important to note that we do this simultaneously. We do not worship in spirit in one setting and truth in another; we are in both at once.

Reflections.

We worship something when we act as if it has value. By nature, human beings are worshippers. Sometimes, we focus our worship on that worthy of reverence (like God). Other times, it is misdirected (for instance, we worship our work, our bank accounts, fashion, or a political icon). No "thing" or "person" is more valuable. The LORD requires true worship **[St. John 4:24]**.

Our spirit is the core of who we are. It is the center of our volition and our emotions. We also know that God is a spiritual being. To worship in spirit is to do something beyond the physical. We do not worship by simply bowing our knees; we worship through a heart posture **[Psalm 51:17]**. Our worship is in line with the worship in heaven **[Psalm 148:1-2; Ephesians 6:12; Revelation 4:8]**.

Worshipping in truth means that we worship based on truth **[Romans 10:2]**. This includes the truth about who God is and what He does, hence why He is worthy of worship. It also consists of the truth about our circumstances. We worship God even when we are experiencing heartache. When we worship Him, we do not forget about our hurt, but we worship even in the truth of our hurt. We also worship in joyful circumstances. Truth can be a means of worship; we worship God when we declare His truth.

To worship God in spirit and truth is to declare that God is worthy of our reverence. We do this through our emotions and our praise. We worship God based on the truth of who He is, the truth of who we are, the truth of what God does, and the truth of what is going on in our world. We do it with a heart inclined toward God and in submission to Him. We worship God when our attitudes, actions, and words declare Him worthy of our actions. "Worthy is the Lamb who was slain to receive power, wealth, wisdom, might, honor and glory and blessing!" **[Revelation 5:12]**.

We war and fight. We become jealous of those who achieve more. We attempt to hinder those we believe have fewer qualifications. We miss the rewards of knowing the gifts and abilities of wonderful people. In some cases, people attack the character of faithful believers, resulting in wounded souls. Why should we contribute to the devil's plots and schemes? Why should our lack of knowing God's word cause us to become delusional and follow those who "pump" us full of false doctrine, resulting in being average?

Satan attacks the souls of true believers. If we focus on giving money, we believe we will always keep our character. Our character is a summation of our attitude, conscience, thoughts, emotions, and intellect. Money will never change character. The devil knows this. Therefore, he emphasizes that we should get more money and receive it the quickest way. God wants us to be wealthy, but to love Him first to receive it. The "money cometh to me now generation" defaults on God's requirement and focuses on the achievement of assets. The "prosperity" movement is satanic in its basic tenets. God gives prosperity when we seek God's Kingdom and righteousness **[St. Matthews 6:33]**.

The way to feed and ultimately change our soul, as outlined in **St. Luke 6:33-36** is to love. When we love people, people will return the love according to what we measure to them.

The receipt will not come in a dribble, but pressed down, shaken together, and running over shall I put into our bosom. Therefore, we see Satan's attacks our souls by twisting the word of God. The chapter of **St. Matthew 4** exemplifies Satan's attempts to wound our souls. A wounded soul is not in touch with God. The devil used money and power, presenting scriptures out of context and in error in his attempt to convince Christ to accept his doctrine.

The wounded soul cannot communicate with God.

Many churches are full of wounded soul. We attempt to get them to praise God during our worship venue and work in the ministry. However, what seem like the lack of interest is a deeper problem. Wounded souls cannot enjoy the good things of God. They cannot rejoice in the blessings of God. Wounded souls are out of step and not in tune with the voice of God. They attend church out of habit or necessity. They develop routines and habits. These habits and routines lack enthusiasm.

The scriptures below reveal to us the consequence of a wounded soul. Let us examine them.

Proverbs 18:14 "The spirit of a man will sustain his infirmity; but a wounded spirit who can bear?"

Proverbs 15:13 "A joyful heart makes a cheerful face, but when the heart is sad, the spirit is broken."

Proverbs 14:10 "The heart knows its own bitterness and a stranger does not share its joy."

Psalm 6:2-4 Have mercy on me, Lord, for I am faint; heal me, Lord, for my bones are in agony. My soul is in deep anguish.

Christians confuse when they feel depressed, offended, rejected, or have other negative feelings with their soul's condition. "Why am I experiencing this after I accepted Jesus into my heart by faith?" In truth, the answer is both simple and yet challenging. Your spirit is 100% regenerated upon believing in Christ and His cross. However, something more is often needed: the healing of soul wounds.

What exactly are soul wounds, and how do they affect us? The answer is this: We have experiences all through our lives. Sometimes, the actions of others hurt us. In addition, we, too, do wrong things. Our sins can leave wounds in us. Additionally, there may be recurring, damaging behaviors from our families. Alcoholism is an example. Those generational behaviors cause pain. Cumulatively, each of these things can leave a mark behind or a measure of damage in your soul.

Some examples of soul wounds.

As a result, when people leave or not accept you in some way in the present, your reaction to them is often an overreaction born out of retained pain. Having been "rejected" before, it can seem reasonable, even self-protective, to not trust and be suspicious now. However, the current situation may not indeed be abandonment or rejection, but the wound in you causes it to be perceived as such. Imagine being tremendously put down as a child, always made to feel inferior and lacking. As an adult, carrying this wound of criticism makes thinking well of yourself difficult. Compliments or praise is often hard to accept. Additionally, celebrating others' successes is a struggle. "Everyone is doing better than I am" thoughts may eat away at peace—and are not true.

All of these (and more) wound our ways of thinking that destroy our quality of life. These wounds affect our relationships. You do not feel safe which makes intimacy difficult because of wound "lenses."

Soul wounds affect your relationship with God.

Most of all, because of soul wounds, your relationship with God and capacity to flourish as a Christian diminish. Being preoccupied with wounds keeps you inwardly focused on repetitive, turbulent, negative thinking. Rather than fully encountering God and receiving all the blessings He has for you, you remain caught up in your ongoing pain and misconceptions. However, do not worry.

All of us go through this to some degree. God wants our healing for the last time. Truly, He wants you healed in mind, soul, and body. The good news is that God wants you to receive healing throughout your being. Now, if any of this sounds familiar to you if you repeatedly feel blue, offended, lonely, or "different from everyone else," you may require some inner healing.

Where do you start?

Sometimes, we embarrass ourselves if we do not have it all together. For example, you may say, "I don't want to admit that I am jealous often." Alternatively, that "I feel lonely and feel like I don't fit in." We often think Christianity is a "stiff upper lip" lifestyle where you must appear that you have it all together, even if you are "dying" inside. This is nonsense. On the contrary, healing and maturing are part of this life. Jesus can heal all things.

God wants you free from these wounds. You do not have to tolerate feeling emotionally out of sorts repeatedly. Besides, the enemy loves this "doorway." When you are struggling with thoughts and emotions, he will throw "fuel on the fire" with whispered lies, exaggerating those moods and then bringing shame because of them.

Christ came to heal the brokenhearted. Jesus said about the Father, *"He has sent me to heal the brokenhearted"* **[Luke 4:18 NKJV].** If someone wounds you, God wants to help. In **Psalm 147:3,** *"[God] heals the heartbroken and bandages their wounds."* We must understand that God wants our souls to prosper. Meditate on the following scripture.

"Beloved, I pray you may prosper in all things and be healthy, just as your soul prospers." 3 John 2 NKJV

The passage above is so fundamental. God wants you to feel safe and whole in your soul. He wants you to concentrate and live joyfully, not constant preoccupation and heaviness. God wants your soul to prosper.

We must pray for God to heal our soul.

Prayer is a two-way conversation with God. That is not the view of religion. The definition of prayer from the original text of the Hebrew bible presents prayer differently and uniquely. The word for prayer in Hebrew is *Tefillah*, which means, *"think out loud."* Prayer is not just informing God of things going on in which we could use his help (He already knows about them anyway). In prayer, we think aloud about God and His goodness. When we think aloud about God's greatness, it builds our faith. Faith cometh by hearing and hearing by the word of God **[Romans 10:17]. Romans 10:17** reveals that faith is not possible by hearing a message or report that we hear.

Paul promised the Spirit would help us as we prayed and often talked to himself about praying "in the Spirit." What exactly does prayer "in the Spirit" mean? Speaking "in the Spirit" means speaking under the guidance of the Spirit as we speak the word of God in prayer. The Holy Spirit helps us by interceding for us **[Romans 8:26]**. No one can say, "Curse Jesus Christ" when speaking "in the Spirit." In addition, no one can say, "Jesus is Lord" (and mean it) unless he is speaking "in the Spirit." Therefore, praying "in the Spirit" involves allowing the Holy Spirit to shape our prayers as we pray.

Praying in the spirit is not speaking in some unknown tongue. This misguided truth minimizes the **TRUTH** and makes some believe they are unique in God. However, when we apply righteous judgment, we can see their lack of faith, study of God's word, and spiritual deficiencies in the fruit of the spirit. The charismatic movement sought to suggest that speaking in Spirit is direct communication with God. If this belief is true, it diminishes Christ's role as Mediator **[I Timothy 2:5]** and High Priest **[Hebrews 4:14-16]**. This false belief also diminishes the role of the Holy Spirit to intercede for us **[Romans 8:26-27]**. This charismatic movement seeks to have some unique relationship with God that is not biblical. They would suggest that anyone who cannot speak in tongues has no relationship with God. However, nowhere in scripture do we find this belief as truth.

The more Scripture you know, the more illumination of God's word by the Holy Spirit can give you regarding various matters. His role is to bring us into remembrance. God has never brought to my mind a scripture I did not know. I know some who claim he has done that for them, but I think the normal way. He works to remember the scriptures we have hidden in our hearts **[Psalms 119:11-16]**. Memorizing Scripture serves to sharpen the Sword of the Spirit. The Bible contains over 8,810 promises. God did not give us the Bible to read but pray through.

As we learned repeatedly throughout this book, by the Spirit of God in prayer is proportionate to our knowledge of the Word of God. Remember, the word is His primary weapon. Paul called the Word of God "the sword of the Spirit!" **(Ephesians 6:17)**

He [the Spirit] guides us in prayer; thus, He helps our infirmities. Nevertheless, the blessed Spirit does more than this; He will often direct the mind to the particular subject of prayer. He dwells within us as our Counselor and points out what we should seek at the hands of God. We do not know why it is so, but we sometimes find our minds carried by a strong undercurrent into a particular line of prayer for some definite purpose. It is not merely that our judgment leads us in that direction, though the Spirit of God usually acts upon us by enlightening our judgment; we often feel an unaccountable and irresistible desire rising within our hearts.

He will guide you both negatively and positively. Negatively, He will forbid you to pray for certain things, just as Paul tried "to go into Bithynia: but the Spirit suffered [him] not" **[Acts 16:7]**. On the other hand, he will cause you to hear a cry within your soul that will guide your petitions, even as He made Paul to listen to the cry from Macedonia, saying, "Come over into Macedonia, and help us" **[Acts 16:9]**.

The condition of our souls matters.

As humans, we focus on our appearance, our style, and our education. While our appearance does provide many benefits and opportunities, our soul matters to God. God's primary concern is spiritual things. We cannot see, hear, or feel spiritual things. However, spiritual things determine our understanding and develop our relationship with God.

Our soul is our "conscious personal self," the "I" that knows itself as "me." Your soul is the identity that makes you who you are. Our soul is our unique self. Our soul is what determines our character. Our heavenly Father spends considerable and deliberate focus on helping us develop our character. In **Mark 8:35- 36,** Jesus says our soul has excellent value. Do you know why this is?

The LORD God formed the man of dust from the ground and breathed the breath of life into his nostrils, and the man became a living soul **[Genesis 2:7]**. Embracing God's creation strategy is important in knowing who you are and why your life is of such great value. God created Adam in two stages. God used a two-steps in the process by which God gave him life. The first step was that God "formed the man of dust from the ground." God formed a body. Now in this way, the man and the woman were similar to the animals: "Now out of the ground the LORD God formed every beast of the field and every bird of the heavens" **[Genesis 2:19]**.

There is a second stage in the creation of Adam, which shows why we are different from animals. The LORD God formed the man of dust from the ground and breathed the breath of life into his nostrils. Then, man became a living soul. In summary, God breathes life into this corpse, making Adam different from the animals. He is more than a body. Adam is a living soul. This soul is capable of knowing God and enjoying God, and it is capable of sinning against God, something the animals cannot do. This is at the heart of what God is saying when he says, "You are made in the image of God" **[Genesis 1:26-27]**. God breathed life into you, and that life will never end.

Apart from the spirit, the body is dead **[James 2:26]**. Think about everything necessary in your life, and you will say, "Where did these things come." Everything you achieve in life, completed in the world, will arise from the soul's life. The devil argued for the body of Moses. However, the devil is not after our bodies. Our body will return to the dust from whence it came **[Ecclesiastes 12:7]**. The devil wants to kill, steal, and destroy our souls. When we sin, our soul sins and adds sin to our character. When we turn a blind eye or ignore a sin, transgression, or iniquity, our souls anchor to those sins. Therefore, our soul is the cause of our sin.

Our temptation comes when lured and enticed by our **desire [James 1:14]**. Where does sin come from? **James 1:14** is a significant verse in the Bible because it tells us how temptation works. Temptation comes to us through the world, the flesh, and the devil. The problem is that it attaches itself to the soul wherever it comes from. If this were not the case, temptation would not be a problem. When temptation comes, the soul receives, retains, embraces, and holds on to it.

Our body goes back to the dust of the ground. Our spirit or emotion is lost in the cemetery. However, the soul goes to God for rendering judgment. Listen to this most familiar scripture. "Do not fear those who kill the body but cannot kill the soul. **[St. Matthews 10:28].** Only God can destroy the soul.

Your life has a beginning, but it does not have an end. One day, you will die, and your body will go back into the ground. However, your soul will last forever. So, "Do not fear those who kill the body, but cannot kill the soul." Your soul has an endless life. That is why it is so important. It is immortal. It has a beginning, but it has no end. We all have a soul. It is inside us. We cannot see it, but it lasts forever. Some of you are actively trying to decide if you are going to follow Christ, knowing that it is costly. You need to know what is at stake. You try to save your life and you lose it. However, Jesus says, "If you lose your life to me, you will save it."

The poor man died and the angels carried him in Abraham's bosom. The rich man also died and was buried, and in Hades, being in torment, he lifted up his eyes and saw Abraham far off and Lazarus at his side **[Luke 16:22-23].**

Our Lord tells the story of two men who died. One of them an Angel carried in Abraham's bosom. Certainly not the poor man's body. That body remained on the earth. So what did the Angel carry to Abraham's side? Not the poor man's body—his soul! Then we read, "The rich man also died and was buried," so everyone knew where *his* grave was. His body placed in a rich man's tomb, with words and dates carved into it. What then was in hades? Not the rich man's body. It was in the tomb. It was the rich man's soul!

The point here is very simple: Death takes life from the body but not from the soul. When you die, your soul goes on to one of two places: One is a place of great joy. The other, according to Jesus, is a place of great torment. In addition, there is a great gulf fixed between them. You cannot get from the one to the other in either direction. There is a heaven to pursue and a hell to avoid. You have a soul: Your soul path - saved or lost. Losing your soul is the ultimate disaster because which you can never recover.

Do you see now why your soul is so valuable? George stood and stared at the wall of his bedroom. Why did he not know of the importance of the soul? He had read Genesis 1, which declared that man became a living soul. He had been in church all his life. He had never heard his pastor or other preachers talk about the importance of the soul. Everyone talks about how one feel in his or her spirit or the Holy Spirit. However, what about the soul? "We have been blind," George said to Susan, Richard, and Cathy. "How does God want us to love Him?" Richard asked. Let us read

St. Luke 10:27. Luke 10:27 is a Bible verse from the New Testament. It is part of a conversation between Jesus and a teacher of the law. The Scripture says,

"He answered, 'Love the Lord your God with all your heart and with all your soul and with all your strength and with your entire mind'; and, 'Love your neighbor as yourself."

"How did we miss this?" George screamed. We focus on loving God and miss the point that we must love Him with our "soul." Richard received the greater revelation. He began to explain to the group. **"St. Luke 10:27** contains a significant teaching from Christ, emphasizing the importance of love for God and one's neighbor." Richard explained, "The verse is part of a conversation where a law teacher asks Jesus about inheriting eternal life. In response, Jesus quotes two commandments."

"Love the Lord your God with all your heart and with all your **"soul"** and with all your strength and with your entire mind." This emphasizes the primary and utmost importance of loving and having devotion to God in every aspect. It speaks to a wholehearted commitment and dedication to a relationship with God. We can only achieve this commandment by allowing our souls to connect with God. "Love your neighbor as yourself": Jesus adds another crucial aspect of love loving others. This commandment highlights the importance of showing love, compassion, and care for those around us. It encourages a selfless and outward-focused love for others, similar to the care one has for oneself.

"How did I miss this?" George sighed. "This is why we fall short of God's glory. We allow our connection with God through our minds. Our minds cannot connect with God. God never speaks to our minds. He always speaks to our soul. God connected our souls to Him. We are God-breathe. He placed a part of Himself in us. God wants to speak and reveal to our souls. Our flesh is filthy, our mind is corrupt, and our senses are deceiving. However, our soul receives the deep things of God."

"We have a lot to think about," George said. "How could we have gone through the motions and missed this valuable point? We can never have intimacy with God without understanding this soul–God relationship. The times we received revelations were because our souls were open to God. A true relationship is about intimacy. True love is not intellectual, physical, or experiential. True love occurs through a soul connection."

Jonathan love for David was a soul connection **[I Samuel 18:1]**. "Can we discuss this verse," Richard asked. I believe this scripture will help accentuate our understanding. How could two men have this kind of soul tie? Perhaps God uses this text as a metaphor for us.

Reflections.

We must not love the LORD with our mind, but with our soul. We must have a soul connection with God. In our mind are fleeting thoughts. However, our soul contains our character, the essence of who we are in God. No thought can contain God. Therefore, He put Himself into our character to assist us in developing Godly Character. There is a difference.

First, the Hebrew word for "love" used here covers a broad range of meanings and does not mean "romantic" or "sexual" love unless the context demands it. Forms of the same word are used for loving God **(Exodus 20:6)**, loving one's neighbor as oneself **(Leviticus 19:18)**, treating foreigners well **(Leviticus 19:34)**, sharing friendship **(Job 19:19)**, having diplomatic ties **(1 Kings 5:1)**, taking pleasure in the work of a subordinate **(1 Samuel 16:21)**, and even "loving" inanimate things **(Proverbs 21:17)**.

Second, David's comparison of his relationship with Jonathan with that of women is probably a reference to his experience with King Saul's daughters. Saul promised one of his daughters for killing Goliath. Saul abruptly gave his first daughter to another man. Saul promised his second daughter, but Saul continued to add conditions to the deal, hoping to see David killed in battle **(1 Samuel 18:17, 25)**. David's loyalty and camaraderie with Jonathan came with no conditions and was of greater value than the companionship with Saul's daughter.

The friendship between David and Jonathan was a covenantal relationship. In **1 Samuel 18:1-5**, we read of David and Jonathan forming an agreement. In this agreement, Jonathan was second in command in David's future reign, and David was to protect Jonathan's family **(1 Samuel 20:16-17, 42; 23:16-18)**.

These two men's relationships possessed at least three qualities.

- First, they sacrificed for one another. In **1 Samuel 18:4,** we read that Jonathan gave David his clothes and military garb. This gift was significant because Jonathan recognized that David would one day be king of Israel. Rather than being envious or jealous, Jonathan submitted to God's will and sacrificed his right to the throne.
- Second, in **1 Samuel 19:1-3,** we read of Jonathan's loyalty toward and defense of David. King Saul told his followers to kill David. Jonathan rebuked his father and recalled David's faithfulness to him in killing Goliath.

- Finally, Jonathan and David were also free to express their emotions with one another. In **1 Samuel 20,** we read of a plan concocted by Jonathan to reveal his father's plans toward David. Jonathan was going to practice his archery. David was safe if he told his servant that the arrows he shot were to the target's side. If Jonathan told his servant that the arrows were beyond the target, David was to leave and not return. Jonathan told the servant that the arrows were beyond the target, meaning David should flee. After releasing his servant, Jonathan found David and the two men cried together.

Clearly, David and Jonathan's relationship went beyond a deep friendship. They did not operate with "lip service." Their relationship was a matter of the soul. This soul connection is what God requires. He does not want us to worship Him with our lips and have our heart and soul far from Him **[St. Matthews 15:8].** What many call love is actual false intimacy. False intimacy is we love what people do, how they make us feel, and what they do for us.

False intimacy refers to a sense of closeness or connection that is not genuine, authentic, or based on a deep understanding of one another. It can manifest in various relationships and contexts, and it often involves a facade of intimacy rather than a true and meaningful connection. Here are a few examples of what false intimacy might look like:

Superficial Connections: Engaging in small talk or surface-level conversations without delving into topics that are more meaningful can create a false sense of intimacy. People may feel like they know each other well, but the connection is only on the surface.

Social Media Friendship: In the age of social media, individuals may curate their online personas to present a carefully crafted image of their lives. People may feel intimately connected to others based on their online presence, but this connection may not reflect the reality of their deeper emotions or experiences.

Emotional Manipulation: Sometimes, individuals may create a false sense of intimacy by manipulating emotions or using emotional tactics to gain trust. This can include insincere empathy or sympathy to elicit a particular response.

Transactional Relationships: Relationships based on transactions or exchanging goods, services, or favors can create a false sense of closeness. The connection is mutually beneficial rather than genuinely understanding each other's thoughts, feelings, and experiences.

Lack of Vulnerability: True intimacy often involves a level of vulnerability where individuals share their authentic selves, including their fears, insecurities, and failures. If one or both parties in a relationship avoid being vulnerable and keep up a facade, it can lead to a false sense of closeness.

Cultivating genuine intimacy requires openness, trust, and a willingness to share both the positive and challenging aspects of oneself. It involves mutual understanding, empathy, and a deep connection beyond surface-level interactions. False intimacy, on the other hand, may provide a temporary illusion of closeness but lacks the substance and authenticity that characterize meaningful relationships.

Richard concluded by saying, "God will also provide revelation for our soul based on soul our connection. Our soul connection determines our level of intimacy. No one teaches us intimacy with God. The church only teaches us about praise, worship, and service. However, if there is no intimacy between God and our soul, we only have false intimacy. George said, "This is so good." Let's get together after Bible Study on Tuesday and examine how to have intimacy with God." Richard, Cathy, Susan, and George walked to Richard's car with a different attitude. They felt that their search to know the God of the Bible was so awesome. They hugged and said goodnight.

Reflection.

God's desire for us is a soul connection. God wants a covenant relationship with us. A covenant relationship goes beyond a marriage. A covenant relationship supersedes the "I Do" of a wedding ceremony. A covenant relationship involves binding promises and relationships. A covenant relationship is the result of Agape love its unconditional.

George and Susan returned to their Family room and collapsed into their favorite chairs. For a moment, they could not speak but stared at each other. Their eyes told their emotions and feelings. As tears rolled down their face, they felt a sense of deliverance. "We are no longer bound to religion, Cathy," George said. "I know George. I feel like a heavy boulder lifted from me, and I realize that our lives have turned from the past into a loving God who only wants a covenant with us, "Susan responded. "Our lives will never be the same. We finally met the God of the Bible and dismissed the God of the church. The God of the church is religion. We will not go back. We can only go forward," George said.

George leaned back, his eyes fixed on Susan as he spoke with conviction. "You know, Susan, for so long, I thought I was serving God, but I realize now that I was serving a system—what I'm calling 'the God of the church.' It was all about rules, rituals, and appearances. I measured my faith by how well I conformed, how often I attended services, or how much I gave. However, when I finally met the God of the Bible—the One who calls us into a real, living relationship with Him— I realized how shallow and empty all that was without Him. The God of the church was religion, but the God of the Bible is life. There is no going back to lifeless rituals once you have experienced the depth of His love and truth. We can only move forward into the fullness of His grace."

Susan nodded, her eyes glistening with understanding. "I know exactly what you mean, George. Religion can create a box that limits how we see God, making Him seem distant or demanding. However, the God of the Bible is so different—He is relational, personal, and compassionate. It is not about what we do to earn His favor but what He has already done for us through Jesus. That changes everything. We are set free when we stop trying to fit God into the constructs of tradition and instead encounter Him through His Word and Spirit. It is like stepping out of the shadows into the light. In addition, once you have tasted that freedom, you cannot settle for anything less. Forward is the only direction that makes sense."

CHAPTER 3

GOING BEYOND PRAISE TO INTIMACY WITH GOD

Intimacy with God is available to every believer. It is as accessible to you as God's promises [2 Corinthians 1:20]. In addition, God's invitation to us is to enjoy intimate fellowship with Him by putting our faith to the test [James 1:2-4]. Let us read this most important scripture.

"My brethren, count it all joy when ye fall into divers' temptations; knowing this, that the trying of your faith worked patience. But let patience have her perfect work, that ye may be perfect and entire, wanting nothing."

A thorough understanding of **James 1:2-4** requires going beyond the surface. On the surface of the scripture, our joy stems from learning patience. A deeper understanding of the Scripture reveals a point of intimacy with God. When we demonstrate patience, we let God know we understand His unconditional love for us. We are not in despair, disillusion, or desperation. Our intimacy with God connects us with God's intention. Suffering should never make us bitter. Our suffering should always make us better.

The heart of intimacy.

Intimacy is what we call the experience of really knowing and someone knowing us. Intimacy involves a mutually consensual relationship where two individuals reciprocate a close, familiar, emotional, and usually affectionate or loving relationship with another person. We frequently use spatial language when describing this experience. An intimate friend is someone we feel very *close* to; they know us deeply. Intimacy is not spatial but relational. We all know how we feel *distant* from someone near us, and we can feel *close* to someone four thousand miles away. God's complaint throughout scripture is that our mouth speaks intimacy, but our hearts are far from Him [Isaiah 29:13].

What makes us feel intimate with God? We cannot have intimacy with a person we do not spend quality time with regularly and consistently. We cannot be intimate with a person we do not trust. Trust is at the heart of intimacy. The more we trust someone, the *closer* we develop a personal and emotional attachment. The degree to which we minimize trust in a relationship is the degree to which intimacy evaporates.

The heart of intimacy with God.

This is as true in our relationship with God as in our relationships with other human beings. Our experience of God's *nearness* or *distance* is not a description of his actual proximity to us but of our experience of intimacy with him. Scripture shows us that God is intimate with those who trust him. The more we trust God, the more intimately we know him. A felt distance from God is often due to a disruption in trust, such as a sin or disappointment.

This reality is vitally important to understand. As Christians, we want to experience intimacy with God. With the psalmist, we say, "For me, it is good to be near God" **[Psalms 73:28]**. In addition, we want to heed James's exhortation and realize its promise: "Draw near to God, and he will draw near to you **[James 4:8]**. However, we can seek that nearness in ways that do not produce it.

Intimacy is more than knowledge.

One common mistake is thinking that nearness to God exists through knowledge accumulation. To know God intimately, we must know crucial things about God. Jesus said, "You will know the truth, and the truth will set you free" **[John 8:32]**, and he pointed out that many worship what they do not know **[John 4:22]**.

However, never in the history of the Christian church has so much theological knowledge been available to so many people as it is today. The American church enjoys perhaps the most significant amount of this abundance. We are awash in Bible translations, good books, insightful articles, recorded sermons, interviews, movies, documentaries, music, and much more. It is suitable for us to be very thankful.

However, America is not abounding in Enoch's (or finding them frequently disappearing) saints who walk with God profoundly intimately **[Genesis 5:24, Hebrews 11:5]**. Why? Because knowledge is not synonymous with trust. That is why Jesus said to the religious leaders of his day, some of whom possessed an encyclopedic knowledge of Scripture,

"You search the Scriptures because you think that in them you have eternal life, and they bear witness about me, yet you refuse to come to me that you may have life." [John 5:39-40].

Biblical knowledge is far better than gold when it fuels our trust in God because it fuels our intimacy with God (Psalm 19:10). However when biblical knowledge replaces our trust in God, it only fuels our pride **[1 Corinthians 8:1]**.

A field of dreams approach.

Another common mistake is achieving intimacy with God through subjective aesthetic experiences. We might call it a "Field of Dreams" approach: If we build the right environment, God will "come." Some pursue this in high liturgical environments designed to inspire an experience of transcendence and mystery. Others pursue it in contemporary worship events designed to encourage an understanding of immanence. Others chase revivals, thinking that proximity to God's power will result in proximity to God. If we truly trust God, such environments can encourage our intimacy with God. However, none inherently possesses the power to conjure God's nearness to us. **"God is impressed with our faith, not our feats."**

Think of it like this: A candlelit dinner with romantic music may encourage a sweet moment between a husband and wife, but only to the degree that the environment encourages and deepens their mutual trust and love. If there is a relational distance between them due to a lack of confidence, the aesthetics cannot bridge the distance. Only restoring the trust will do that.

How we draw near to God.

The Bible reveals the secret to drawing near to God and having him draw near to us. We draw near to God through faith in Christ, who gives us access to him [**Hebrews 4:14–16; 7:25; Philippians 3:9**]. We put our trust in "his precious and very great promises," which find their Yes in Christ. We impress God with our faith, not our feats. Where trust is lacking, we are not pleased with the quantity of our knowledge or the quality of our aesthetic events. "And without faith, it is impossible to please him, for whoever would draw near to God must believe that he exists and that He rewards those who seek Him."

When God sees someone whose heart fully trusts His promises and lives by them, God comes to support that saint **(2 Chronicles 16:9)** strongly and manifests himself to him:

"Whoever has my commandments and keeps them, he it is who loves me. And my Father will love him who loves me, and I will love him and manifest myself to Him." God desires that we know Him, build a relationship, and spend eternity with Him.

This is why He has given us access to Himself through Jesus. Salvation is our open door for encountering God. Jesus's sacrifice on the cross grants us free access to know Him more. The truth we need to remember is that Almighty God, who made heaven and earth, wants to be in a relationship with us and wants us to know Him the way He understands us. He sees every effort we push to grow in intimacy with Him. In addition, we can trust that He will draw near to us when we draw near to Him.

Practical steps toward intimacy.

In addition, Jesus told them, "I am the bread of life. He who comes to me shall never hunger, and he who believes in me shall never thirst." God gave us a clear picture of what He is like, and He put it all down in a book that we can use to learn and remind ourselves of His nature. In the Bible, we see how God interacts with man, communicates, and the topics He sees as priorities. "If we want to know God more deeply and draw closer to His heart, then we need to spend time in His word consistently daily," says Jon Throw, singer, songwriter, and IHOPKC worship leader. "If we don't feed ourselves with the Word of God on the inside, we fail to feed our soul."

Jesus refers to Himself as the living water and the Word. As we read Scripture about Him, we learn what He is like and how He thinks. We come to a greater understanding of His character. At the same time, He renews, refreshes, and washes us with the water of the Word. We begin to think about how He feels.

Worship.

God is Spirit, and those who worship Him must worship in spirit and truth. **(John 4:24)**

In worship, we declare the truth of who the Lord is. Through prayer, we align our will to God's desire and can reset our focus on the One who is our Maker, Creator, and LORD. As we worship, we should see God the One with all power and authority, compassionate and sovereign over every part of our lives and this world. We should gain a greater understanding of God and know who He is. When that occurs, we change our perspective of others, our circumstances, and ourselves from the correct vantage point.

More than a song, worship is the way we respond to God's gift of His life for us. Consequently, we are entirely free and can live with Him forever.

Prayer

The Lord asked us to communicate with Him to grow closer to Him. Unlike a dated, stagnant ritual of speaking words to the air, prayer is a conversation in which we talk to God, and He responds. This conversation strengthens us, helps focus us, and brings us greater fellowship with our Maker. As with our closest friends and family members, the more we speak to God, the more we learn His character. Prayer is a critical factor in our relationship with God. Our God is living and active in the lives of His creation every day. He desires that we be children who know Him and collaborate with Him in the work of the Kingdom to bring His good plans for our lives and those around us.

Journaling.

Many times in the Bible, the Lord's followers memorialized physical locations to remind themselves and others of the great things God had done in their lives. Although we may not put up national monuments daily to express the Lord's faithful work in our lives, it is essential to take time and reflect on the Lord's faithfulness.

Times of reflection help produce gratitude in our hearts now and can strengthen us in difficult times of trials and tribulation. When we record how the Lord prevailed in our times of sickness, need, or fear, we catalog His work and the testimony of His conquering power in our lives.

We genuinely become living epistles that not only know the history of God's display of strength and compassion in everyday situations but also retain those memories of what our Father has done, enabling us to encourage others to overcome in their time of trial **[Revelation 21:7].** We can point to the One who is faithful and accurate and help them draw closer to God on their path toward greater intimacy.

God's invitation to intimacy.

God wants intimacy with you. Christ has done all the hard work on the cross to make it possible. All He requires is that you believe in Him. He wants you to trust Him wholeheartedly **[Proverbs 3:5].** This means that his invitation to you to enjoy intimacy with Him is the providence in your life that tests your faith. What you must trust God most for right now is what He means for you to draw closer to Him. It is likely an invitation that your flesh wants to decline. However, as you read your Bible, the great cloud of witnesses agrees with James and Peter. The most significant testing of faith is the path to the greatest joy. In addition, do they not agree with Paul that it is not worth comparing to the pleasure of knowing Christ and the coming glory? True Intimacy with God often occurs in the places where we must trust Him most. Heaven on earth is the inexpressible joy and peace that completely surpasses understanding from trusting God. The old hymn writer said, "They who trust him wholly find Him true."

As George received this revelation, he began to understand what was missing. His whole life, he focused on praise. Now, he understood that true worship involves intimacy. His entire life, teachers instructed him to praise God. The church taught him to worship God in Spirit and truth. He understands that praise and worship are incomplete until we have true intimacy. Glorifying God without intimacy is a form of godliness but denying the power thereof. We sit in church and listen to the music ministry and a sermon. Then, we acknowledge that we have had a good church service. The truth is that our behavior before church defines our behavior in church. We should already have the spirit of praise, George thought.

It was Thursday night; as their tradition, it was private and personal devotion. George and Susan would study the Bible, pray, and praise. However, this Thursday night would be different. George realized that true intimacy with God is a lifelong journey that requires patience, dedication, and openness to growth. Each person's path is unique, and finding the practices and approaches that resonate most deeply with you is essential. There is a way to approach God that gains God's attention. Before he went into their prayer room, George pondered. How do we get God's attention to develop a relationship that leads to intimacy? There has to be more intimacy with God than we experience at church. He believed his relationship would become intimate if He could gain God's attention. How do we seek and gain God's attention, George thought.

Seeking God's attention deepens one's spiritual connection and ensures God notices our prayers and efforts. After deep thought, George developed thirteen steps and practices that draw God's attention and favor:

Sincere Prayer: Pray with sincerity and a genuine heart. Your words are as important as the intention and emotion behind them. Speak to God honestly and openly, sharing your genuine thoughts and feelings.

Repentance and Humility: Acknowledge your sins and shortcomings and seek forgiveness. Approach God with a humble heart, recognizing your need for His grace and mercy.

Obedience and Faithfulness: Live according to God's commandments and teachings. Show your faith through your actions and strive to live a life that reflects your beliefs and values.

Worship and Praise: Regularly engage in acts of prayer and praise. Worship is simply doing and serving God. Worship is more than attending religious services. Worship expresses our gratitude for God's blessings through our efforts.

Fasting and Sacrifice: Participate in fasting or other forms of sacrifice to demonstrate your devotion and discipline. These acts can help you focus more on spiritual matters and less on worldly concerns.

Service to Others: Show love and compassion through service and charity. Many religious traditions teach that serving others is a way to serve God and earn His favor.

Study and Meditation: Spend time studying the Bible to receive revelations. Reflect on God's word and seek to understand His will for your life.

Consistency and Perseverance: Be consistent in your spiritual practices, and do not give up, even when you feel distant from God. Perseverance in your faith journey is a sign of devotion.

Community and Fellowship: Engage with a community of believers. Sharing your spiritual journey with others can provide support and encouragement and help you stay focused on your faith.

Seek Guidance: Consult with spiritual leaders or mentors who can offer wisdom and advice on your spiritual journey. They can help you identify areas for growth and improvement.

Nature and Reflection: Spend time contemplating God's creation in nature. Many people feel a stronger connection to God when the beauty and majesty of the natural world surround them.

Gratitude: Cultivate an attitude of gratitude. Regularly thank God for the blessings in your life, and focus on the positive aspects of your existence.

Remember, these practices are not about earning God's attention or favor through merit alone but developing a more profound, sincere relationship with Him. They are about aligning your life with God's will and being open to His presence and guidance.

George and Susan sat quietly while they reminisced about their new knowledge. In one respect, they were grateful for this divine revelation. However, they struggled with their egos because of their lack of understanding. They took pride in being faithful to God, His Son, and Holy Spirit. Now, they realized they had only scratched the surface. So many years in a place of inadequate understanding. They realized they had a form of godliness. However, they were grateful for God's grace and mercy. The LORD gave them time to discover the God of the Bible. They now understood that the God of the Bible differed from the God of the church.

"I never start anything without finishing it," George said. "Let's go to bed, honey. Susan said I am excited to see what we learn next week at church. Okay, Susan, I need to rest my mind. Please pray that I go to sleep. I feel so bound in knots."

CHAPTER 4

GOD'S PURPOSE FOR REVELATIONS

George often visited his prayer room. It was his place to meditate, study, and pray. He sat in the room staring at the bible lying on his study desk. His recent revelations profoundly affected him the last couple of weeks. He was convinced of his strong relationship with God. Unfortunately, he discovered he was using the wrong measuring tape. He measured his relationship with God based on "things." So, was his life of favor based on his intimacy with God, or was it simply the grace of God? He understood the scripture better: "What profit a man to gain the whole world and lose his soul [St. Mark 8:36].

What is favor without a revelation? George thought. The favor of God, in the absence of a specific revelation, is God's provision of divine grace. God's grace manifests in blessings, opportunities, protection, inner peace, thriving relationships, and unexpected provision. While a revelation offers clarity and direct communication from the Divine, the process of revelation transcends the ordinary human capacity for understanding and insight. Prophets, messengers, or chosen individuals typically receive divine revelations. However, divine revelations are available to all believers.

Tears fell from George's eyes and rolled down his cheeks as he thought about how he could have died and not known that there was a deeper place in God's mind. Psalms 91 became clearer. He that dwells in the secret place of the Almighty shall abide under the shadow of the Almighty [Psalms 91:1]. The "secret place" is God's thoughts. George began to pray and ask for wisdom to understand.

The Bible is the ultimate source of divine revelation, containing God's communication to humanity. George felt a nudge to discover the profound purpose of God's revelation as depicted in the Bible, delving into critical scriptures illuminating God's divine intent. George discovered four primary purposes for why God provides revelations to man.

Divine Guidance and Moral Direction: Both the Old and New Testaments display instances where God reveals His will to guide humanity morally and ethically. In the Old Testament, the Ten Commandments, given to Moses on Mount Sinai [Exodus 20:1-17]; exemplify God's desire to provide a clear moral framework for His people. These commandments encompass principles such as honoring parents, abstaining from murder and theft, and avoiding false witness, emphasizing the importance of ethical conduct in alignment with God's divine standards.

In the New Testament, Jesus Christ's teachings further elucidate God's moral guidance. In the Sermon on the Mount [St. Matthews 5-7], Jesus expounds on ethical principles, challenging conventional norms and highlighting the essence of righteousness. The revelation in these scriptures serves not only to instruct but also to inspire believers to embody virtues like humility, mercy, and peacemaking.

Establishing a Relationship with the Divine: The Bible portrays God's revelations as a means of documenting and nurturing a relationship between the Creator and His creation. God walked and talked with Adam and Eve in the Garden of Eden, fostering a close communion **[Genesis 3:8]**. However, when sin entered the world, sin disrupted this direct relationship. Throughout the Bible, God initiates various forms of revelation to restore and deepen the connection between Himself and humanity. The prophet Isaiah speaks of God's desire for a relationship, saying, "Come now and let us settle the matter. Though your sins are like scarlet, they shall be as white as snow" **[Isaiah 1:18 NIV]**. This invitation encapsulates the redemptive nature of God's revelations, offering forgiveness and restoration to those who turn to Him.

Preservation of Truth and Wisdom: The Bible is not merely a historical document but a repository of eternal truths and divine wisdom. God's revelations depict as a means of preserving and transmitting these truths across generations declare, "All your words are true; all your righteous laws are eternal." This underscores the timeless nature of God's revelations, which endure as an unwavering source of truth.

The Apostle Paul emphasizes the role of scripture in providing wisdom and instruction: "All Scripture is God-breathed and is useful for teaching, rebuking, correcting, and training in righteousness" **[2 Timothy 3:16 NIV]**. This divine inspiration ensures that the Bible remains a guide for believers, offering principles that transcend cultural and temporal boundaries.

Testing and Strengthening Faith: The Bible portrays God's revelations as a means of preparing and strengthening the faith of His people. Abraham's journey is a poignant example of such strengthening. In **Genesis 22**, God instructs Abraham to sacrifice his son Isaac, a command that challenges the very core of Abraham's faith. Yet, as Abraham demonstrates unwavering obedience, God provides a ram for the sacrifice and reaffirms His covenant with Abraham **[Genesis 22:14]**.

The Apostle James reflects on the purpose of trials in the Christian life, stating, "Consider it pure joy, my brothers and sisters, whenever you face trials of many kinds because you know that the strengthening of your faith produces perseverance" **[James 1:2-3 NIV]**. God's revelations, often accompanied by challenges, refine and strengthen believers' faith, fostering a reliance on God and a deeper understanding of His providence. The biblical scriptures provide a rich tapestry of God's purpose for revelation, encompassing divine guidance, establishing a relationship with the Creator, preserving eternal truths, and testing and strengthening faith. Through the pages of the Bible, believers encounter a God who actively communicates His will, offering a roadmap for righteous living and an invitation to an intimate relationship. As Christians reflect on the scriptures, they find guidance for their present circumstances and a timeless source of wisdom that transcends the boundaries of time and culture. In the revelation of God, believers discover a purposeful and transformative journey toward a deeper understanding of their Creator and His divine plan for their lives.

The Benefits of Receiving Divine Revelation. The concept of divine revelation is a cornerstone, providing believers with a unique and profound connection to the sacred. The Bible is the ultimate source of God's revelations, containing insights, guidance, and promises that shape the lives of believers. This author seeks to delve into the benefits of receiving God's revelations, exploring how these divine disclosures, as depicted in the Scriptures, bring about transformation, assurance, wisdom, and a deeper understanding of God's purpose and plans.

Transformation of Character: As conveyed through the Bible, God's revelations will transform individuals' character. The Apostle Paul, in his letter to the Romans, emphasizes the renewing of the mind through God's truth: "Do not conform to the pattern of this world but be transformed by the renewing of your mind. Then you can test and approve God's will, His good, pleasing and perfect will" **[Romans 12:2 NIV]**.

The renewal of the mind is a transformative process as believers immerse themselves in God's revelations. The Scriptures provide moral guidelines and a profound understanding of God's nature and redemptive plan. As individuals, engage with these revelations, their perspectives shift, aligning more closely with God's will and fostering the development of virtues such as love, patience, and humility.

Assurance and Hope: God's revelations offer believers assurance and hope, especially in times of trial and uncertainty. The Psalmist declares, "Your word is a lamp for my feet, a light on my path" **[Psalm 119:105].** This metaphor underscores the illuminating effect of God's revelations, providing clarity and guidance amid life's challenges.

The Apostle Peter echoes this sentiment, emphasizing the reliability of God's promises: "His divine power has given us everything we need for a godly life through our knowledge of him who called us by his glory and goodness" **[2 Peter 1:3]**. Through God's revelations, believers find a firm foundation for their faith, a source of unwavering hope that transcends the transient nature of earthly circumstances.

Wisdom for Decision-Making: The Scriptures are replete with instances where God's revelations provide wisdom for decision-making. King Solomon, renowned for his wisdom, attributes his discernment to God's guidance. **Proverbs 2:6**: "For the Lord gives wisdom; from his mouth come knowledge and understanding."

God's revelations in the Bible serve as a comprehensive guide for navigating the complexities of life. Whether facing moral dilemmas, relational challenges, or existential questions, believers can turn to the Scriptures for divine wisdom. The Apostle James encourages seeking God's guidance in decision-making, stating, "If any of you lacks wisdom, you should ask God, who gives generously to all without finding fault, and it will be given to you" **[James 1:5]**.

Deepening Relationship with God: Receiving God's revelations fosters a deeper and more intimate relationship between our Creator and us. Jesus, in His prayer for His disciples, expresses the profound unity He desires with them: "I have given them the glory that you gave me, that they may be one as we are one I in them and you in me so that they may be brought to complete unity" **[John 17:22- 23]**.

The Bible portrays God's revelations as a means of drawing humanity closer to Him. As believers engage with the Scriptures, they encounter the heart of God, His love, and His desire for communion. The Apostle Paul, in his letter to the Ephesians, prays for believers to have a deep understanding of God's love, rooted in revelation: "I pray that out of his glorious riches, He may strengthen you with power through His Spirit in your inner being, so that Christ may dwell in your hearts through faith. And I pray that you, being rooted and established in love, may have power, together with all the Lord's holy people, to grasp how wide and long and high and deep is the love of Christ" **[Ephesians 3:16-18]**.

Empowerment for Service: God's revelations empower believers to live lives of service and purpose. The Prophet Isaiah, upon receiving a vision of God's glory, responds with willingness and readiness for divine commission: "Then I heard the voice of the Lord saying, 'Whom shall I send? And who will go for us?' And I said, 'Here am I. Send me!'" **[Isaiah 6:8]**.

Throughout the Bible, individuals who receive God's revelations often find themselves called to a specific purpose. Moses, Jonah, Esther, and the apostles, upon receiving divine guidance, embark on missions that impact history. God's revelations clarify His will and imbue believers with the strength and conviction to fulfill their unique calling.

A Source of Comfort and Encouragement: The Scriptures portray God's revelations as a source of comfort and encouragement during distress. In times of trouble, the psalmist turns to God's promises: "When anxiety was great within me, your consolation brought me joy" **[Psalm 94:19]**. The Apostle Paul, facing challenges in his ministry, finds solace in God's assurances: "But the Lord stood at my side and gave me strength" **[2 Timothy 4:17]**.

God's revelations offer a comforting assurance of His presence and faithfulness. In times of sorrow, doubt, or despair, believers find solace in the promises in the Scriptures. The Apostle Paul, in his letter to the Romans, expresses confidence in God's unshakable love. "For I am convinced that neither death nor life, neither angels nor demons, neither the present nor the future, nor any powers, neither height nor depth nor anything else in all creation, will be able to separate us from the love of God that is in Christ Jesus our Lord" **[Romans 8:38-39]**.

The benefits of receiving God's revelations, as depicted in the Scriptures, extend far beyond mere information or guidance. These divine disclosures can transform character, provide assurance and hope, offer wisdom for decision-making, deepen the relationship between believers and God, empower for service, and serve as a source of comfort and encouragement. As believers engage with the Bible, they discover a rich tapestry of divine communication that shapes their identity, purpose, and understanding of the Creator. In the reception of God's revelations, believers find guidance for the present and a timeless source of wisdom and assurance that transcends life's challenges.

Why would anyone be content with a superficial understanding of God's word and never attempt to go deeper in understanding the character of God? The Scriptures abound with teachings that challenge believers to transcend the status quo and resist the temptation to conform unthinkingly to societal norms. This call to a higher standard is a recurring theme throughout the Bible, urging individuals not to become satisfied with mere adherence to the world's expectations. Instead, it encourages a transformative journey towards a life guided by divine principles, often in direct contrast to the patterns of the world.

The Apostle Paul, in his letter to the Romans, delivers a poignant message about the transformative power of renewing one's mind and resisting conformity to the world: "Do not conform to the pattern of this world but be transformed by the renewing of your mind. Then you can test and approve God's will his good, pleasing, and perfect will" **[Romans 12:2]**. This verse underscores the dichotomy between conformity and transformation. Conformity often involves adopting society's prevailing attitudes, behaviors, and values without critical examination. On the contrary, transformation implies a radical change, a renewal of the mind that enables individuals to discern and align themselves with God's divine will. By resisting conformity, believers open themselves to a life of purpose and spiritual insight.

In his first epistle, the Apostle John provides further insight into the dangers of conformity, cautioning against you will die, attachment to the world's ways: "Do not love the world or anything in the world. If anyone loves the world, love for the Father is not in them" **[1 John 2:15]**. This verse emphasizes the incompatibility of a love for the world with a genuine love for God. It serves as a stark reminder that aligning oneself too closely with worldly desires, values, and pursuits can lead to spiritual estrangement from God. The call to resist conformity prioritizes a love for the divine over an attachment to temporal, worldly pursuits.

Jesus, in His teachings, often highlighted the distinction between the narrow and wide paths. In the Gospel of Matthew, He instructs His followers to choose the narrow path, cautioning against the allure of the broad road that leads to destruction: "Enter through the narrow gate. For wide is the gate, broad is the road that leads to destruction, and many enter through it. But small is the gate, and narrow is the road that leads to life, and only a few find it" **[St. Matthews 7:13-14]**.

The Apostle Paul, in his letter to the Ephesians, urges believers not only to resist conformity but also to renounce the unfruitful deeds of darkness actively: "Have nothing to do with the fruitless deeds of darkness, but rather expose them" **[Ephesians 5:11]**.

This warning goes beyond a passive rejection of conformity; it advocates an active stance against practices contrary to God's will. Jesus instructed us to resist the status quo and confront the darkness, contributing to a transformative influence on the world rather than succumbing to its adverse impacts.

The Apostle Paul's letter to the Colossians instructs us to maintain a perspective that transcends earthly concerns: "Since, then, you have been raised with Christ, set your hearts on things above, where Christ is, seated at the right hand of God. Set your minds on things above, not earthly things" **[Colossians 3:1-2]**. This scripture encourages believers to shift their focus from the temporal and fleeting concerns of the world to the eternal and transcendent realities of God's kingdom. By positioning their minds on things above, individuals can resist the gravitational pull of conformity to the world's values and align themselves with a higher, divine perspective.

The Old Testament, particularly in the book of Isaiah, echoes the call to separation from worldly influences **[Isaiah 52:11]**. "Depart, depart, and go out from there! Touch not any unclean thing! Come out from it and be pure, you who carry the articles of the Lord's house." This call to separation emphasizes the need for believers to distance themselves from impurity and ungodliness. The language is powerful, urging a decisive departure from conformity to the world's standards and an active commitment to holiness.

The biblical perspective on resisting conformity is a powerful call to a transformative and counter-cultural way of life. The Scriptures consistently emphasize the need to transcend the status quo, resist the pull of worldly values, and embrace a higher, divine perspective. Whether through the renewing of the mind, the rejection of earthly desires, the choice of the narrow path, the active renunciation of worldly trends, the setting of minds on things above, or the call to separation, the Bible provides a rich tapestry of teachings that guide believers away from conformity and towards a life aligned with God's purpose. In embracing this transcendent mindset, individuals embark on a journey reflecting God's Word transformative power in their lives.

George and Richard held their usual Thursday get together. They would meet and relax discussing politics, football, or any other relevant topic. This time was moments to unwind and fellowship. Most of what they said was not serious. However, this Thursday was different. Their new revelations had them speechless.

George was speechless about his new revelation because it was unlike anything he had ever experienced before. The overwhelming clarity of how the Holy Spirit worked to unveil Christ to him left him in awe. He felt as though the Holy Spirit lifted a veil from his eyes, and for the first time, he saw the profound depth of God's love and the centrality of Christ in every aspect of his life. The thought that the Spirit had been patiently working in him, even in his moments of doubt and wandering, humbled him to the core. George struggled to find words to express the magnitude of this truth, overwhelmed by the weight of God's grace and the Holy Spirit's intimate involvement in his journey of faith.

George sat in quiet contemplation, his heart full but his words failing him. The magnitude of the truth he had encountered—that God's primary concern is the soul—was almost too much to bear. He felt an overwhelming sense of humility as he considered how deeply God valued something so fragile yet eternal within him. The weight of this realization pressed upon him, not as a burden but as a profound call to gratitude. Every moment of his life, every struggle, and every triumph seemed now to point toward this divine focus on his soul's eternal state. It was not just an abstract idea; it was a deeply personal revelation that God's grace had intimately woven into every step of his journey.

As George meditated further, he became acutely aware of the Holy Spirit's role in bringing him to this point of understanding. The Spirit who had convicted him in moments of sin, comforted him in seasons of loss, and guided him when the path ahead seemed unclear. George realized that the Holy Spirit's work was not merely to improve his external circumstances but to shape and sanctify his soul for God's purposes. This realization brought tears to his eyes as he grasped the profound intimacy of God's involvement in his life. The Creator of the universe cared enough to dwell within him, molding him from the inside out.

This revelation left George with a renewed sense of purpose and responsibility. He felt called to nurture his soul with the same care and intention that God showed toward it. He resolved to immerse himself in Scripture, prayer, and fellowship, knowing by which his soul could remain aligned with God's will. More importantly, George felt compelled to share this truth with others—not as a preacher dispensing knowledge but as a fellow traveler inviting others to experience the depth of God's grace. His struggle to find words now felt less like a limitation and more like an acknowledgment of the infinite nature of God's love—a love that words could scarcely contain.

CHAPTER 5

IT'S ALL ABOUT HOW YOU READ IT

It was Sunday, and as George and Susan always did, they went to church. George could not stop thinking about his newfound insight into the revelations of God. His expectations of Pastor Howell were higher today. He expected to receive insight into the character and purpose of God for his life. As usual, the music ministry set the people's attitude for the word. What unique insight will Pastor Howell give us today?

Pastor Howell gave his usual uplifting sermon. It was another "feel good" moment. Everyone nodded in agreement to Pastor Howell's three-point and a close. George had not noticed that Pastor Howell read from a manuscript for some reason. He remembered reading about "Rhema" and "Logos." His realization made him wonder about Pastor Howell preaching style. Was Pastor Howell preaching Rhema or Logos? Rhema is a Greek word that means spoken word. The Greek term "Rhema" used in the New Testament refers to a spoken word or a word revealed in a specific context. George wondered if reading from a manuscript hindered the delivery of a Rhema word.

Rhema and Logos differ because Rhema is a word or utterance from God spoken to an individual in a particular situation or context. In contrast, Logos refers to the general message or Word of God. For example, when you read the Bible, which is the logos of God, you may come across a verse that speaks to your heart and applies to your current situation. That verse becomes a Rhema word for you, a personal and instant speaking of God. The Rhema word can guide, comfort, or correct you, depending on what you average at that moment. A Rhema word consistent with the Logos word, but it is more specific and timely.

In biblical language, the terms "Rhema" and "Logos" stand as pillars, each carrying unique nuances that contribute to the depth and richness of Scripture. While both words translate as "words" in English, understanding the difference between Rhema and Logos is crucial for grasping the layers of meaning within the biblical text. This author aims to explore the distinctions between Rhema and Logos, drawing on scriptural references to illuminate their significance in the context of divine communication and revelation.

"Logos" holds a profound and foundational place in Greek philosophy and Christian theology. In Greek philosophy, Logos signifies a principle of order and knowledge, an underlying reason that governs the cosmos. In the New Testament, especially in the Gospel of John, the concept of Logos takes on a distinctly Christian significance.

St. John 1:1-3 unfolds with the majestic declaration: "In the beginning was the Word [Logos], and the Word was with God, and the Word was God. He was with God in the beginning. Through him, all things were made; without him, nothing was made that has been made." This profound introduction to the Gospel establishes the pre-existence and divinity of the Logos, identifying Him as the creative force behind the cosmos.

The Logos identifies with Christ Himself. **St. John 1:14** continues, "The Word became flesh and made his dwelling among us. We have seen his glory, the glory of the one and only Son, who came from the Father, full of grace and truth." Here, the Logos is not merely a principle but a person Jesus Christ, the incarnate Son of God. The Logos, therefore, represents God's eternal, divine expression, embodying His wisdom, creative power, and redemptive purpose. The cosmic, overarching plan of God finds its ultimate fulfillment in Christ.

Unlike Logos' all-encompassing and eternal nature, "Rhema" refers to a specific spoken word or utterance. Rhema carries the idea of a word that is timely, relevant, and applicable to a particular situation or moment. While Logos encapsulates the divine plan and purpose, Rhema zooms in on God's specific, spoken communication to individuals. One notable instance of Rhema in the New Testament is in **St. Luke 1:38** when Mary responds to the angel Gabriel's announcement of her miraculous conception: "I am the Lord's servant. May your word [Rhema] to me be fulfilled." Here, Rhema represents the specific message or promise spoken by the angel to Mary a word directed toward her at that particular moment.

Another example occurs in **St. Matthew 4:4** during Christ Jesus' temptation in the wilderness: "Jesus answered, 'it is written: "Man shall not live on bread alone, but on every word [Rhema] that comes from the mouth of God."'" In this context, Rhema emphasizes the immediate, spoken response of God a timely and specific word that sustains and guides. **Ephesians 6:17** further highlights the distinction between Logos and Rhema, where the verse describes the armor of God. "Take the helmet of salvation and the sword of the Spirit, which is the word [Rhema] of God." Here, Rhema represents the specific, spoken word of God that believers wield as a weapon in their spiritual warfare.

While Logos and Rhema convey distinct aspects of divine communication, they are not mutually exclusive. Instead, they work harmoniously to reveal the comprehensive and personal nature of God's communication with humanity. In **2 Timothy 3:16-17**, the apostle Paul affirms the unity of Logos and Rhema in the context of Scripture: "All Scripture is God-breathed and is useful for teaching, rebuking, correcting and training in righteousness, so that the servant of God may be thoroughly equipped for every good work." As the written Logos, the entire Scripture encompasses the breathed-out, specific words (Rhema) that are timely and applicable to various aspects of believers' lives.

Hebrew 4:12 exemplifies the relationship between Logos and Rhema. "For the word [Logos] of God is alive and active. Sharper than any double-edged sword, it penetrates even to dividing soul and spirit, joints and marrow; it judges the thoughts and attitudes of the heart." The Logos penetrates and discerns precisely as the living and active Word, manifesting itself in timely Rhema as needed.

Another way to understand the interplay between Logos and Rhema is to consider the spoken and written aspects of God's communication. The Logos often associates with the written Word of God Scripture while Rhema is connected with God has spoken, living communication in specific situations. **Romans 10:17** captures the essence of the relationship between faith and the spoken Rhema: "Consequently, faith comes from hearing the message, and the message is heard through the word [Rhema] about Christ." Our faith ignites and sustains through the specific, spoken messages about Christ the Rhema that individuals hear.

In contrast, **James 1:22-23** emphasizes the transformative power of the Logos when applied: "Do not merely listen to the word [Logos], and so deceive yourselves. Do what it says. Anyone who listens to the word [Logos] but does not do what it says is like someone who looks at his face in a mirror." Here, the Logos is something heard and applied—a guiding principle for life.

Faith and obedience characterizes our response to Rhema. When God speaks a specific word into a situation, our faith requires belief and acts upon that utterance. Obedience to a timely Rhema often leads to unfolding God's purposes and realizing His promises. Abraham's response to God's Rhema serves as a powerful example. In **Genesis 22:2**. God provides a specific, spoken command: "Take your son, your only son, whom you love—Isaac—and go to the region of Moriah. Sacrifice him there as a burnt offering on a mountain I will show you." Abraham's faith-filled obedience to this Rhema demonstrates the transformative power of responding to God's specific words.

Similarly, the Virgin Mary's response to the angel's Rhema in **St. Luke 1:38** reflects a posture of faith and obedience: "I am the Lord's servant. May your word [Rhema] to me be fulfilled." Mary's willingness to embrace God's specific, spoken word sets in motion the birth of a Savior who would redeem the world.

George sought a preached word that would provide living communication of God in specific situations. "Gaining Biblical knowledge is important," George said. However, George did not attend church for entertainment. He understood the value of the church. Without a church, we could not experience corporate praise, ministry, fellowship, evangelism, and discipleship. However, we are only going through the motions unless we receive Rhema.

George understood the principle of not judging others. His issue was not judgment but rather getting clarity. How could he identify the difference between Rhema, revelations, false prophets, and performers? George never claimed the gift of discernment. He usually felt inspired by the atmosphere. However, in this season, he sought more clarity, a more profound revelation, and a more robust relationship with God. Things could not operate as usual. "We must stay on task, Susan," George said. "I am with you all the way," Susan responded. George gently urged Susan to stay on task, emphasizing the importance of seeking understanding in the revelations meant to nourish her soul. He explained that distractions, though often subtle, could pull her away from the profound truths God was unveiling through His Word and Spirit. With a compassionate tone, George reminded her that these revelations were not merely intellectual exercises but life-giving insights designed to transform her heart and deepen her relationship with Christ. "Susan," he said, "this is about more than knowledge it's about aligning your spirit with God's will and discovering His peace and purpose for you. Stay focused, and let the Holy Spirit guide you into all truth.

Reflection.

Another way to understand the interplay between Logos and Rhema is to consider the spoken and written aspects of God's communication. Logos are often associated with the written Word of God Scripture while Rhema connects with God's spoken, living communication in specific situations.

CHAPTER 6

THE THIN LINE

In the realm of spirituality and religious experience, the thin line between genuine revelations, false prophets, or performers is a subject of perennial concern. The desire for divine guidance, insight, and a connection with the supernatural has led individuals to seek revelations, but discerning the authenticity of such experiences is paramount. We must explore the delicate balance between revelations and false prophets, examining biblical principles, historical instances, and practical guidelines to help individuals navigate this complex concept.

The Bible provides a framework for understanding the nature of true revelations and the dangers posed by false prophets. In the Old Testament, **Deuteronomy 18:20-22** serves as a stern warning about false prophets: "But a prophet who presumes to speak in my name anything I have not commanded, or a prophet who speaks in the name of other gods, is to be put to death. You may say to yourselves, 'How can we know when the Lord has not spoken a message?' If what a prophet or preacher proclaims in the name of the Lord does not take place or come true, that is a message the Lord has not spoken." This passage underscores the severe consequences of false prophecy and provides a practical criterion for discernment. The reliability of a prophet's message ties to its fulfillment; if what the prophet prophesies does not happen, it is a clear sign that the prophet has spoken presumptuously.\

In the New Testament, Christ Jesus Himself warns of false prophets in **Matthew 7:15-16** "Watch out for false prophets. They come to you in sheep's clothing, but inwardly, they are ferocious wolves. By their fruit, you will recognize them." Here, Jesus emphasizes the importance of discerning the character and the outcomes of the teachings of those who claim to be prophets. Like healthy trees, true prophets bear good fruit, while false prophets produce fruit that exposes their deceptive nature.

Throughout history, various religious movements grapples with the challenges posed by false prophets. The early Christian church faced the issue of false teachings and deceptive leaders, leading the apostles to guide discernment. In **1 John 4:1**, the apostle John advises believers, "Dear friends, do not believe every spirit, but test the spirits to see whether they are from God because many false prophets have gone out into the world." The Apostle Paul, in his farewell address to the Ephesian elders in **Acts 20:28-30**, expresses concern about the emergence of false teachers from within the Christian community: "Keep watch over yourselves and all the flock of which the Holy Spirit has made you overseers. Be shepherds of the church of God, which he bought with His blood.

Understanding the characteristics of false prophets is crucial for discernment. In addition to the biblical warnings, various passages provide insights into the traits of deceptive leaders.

"I know that after I leave, savage wolves will come among you and not spare the flock. Even from your number, men will arise and distort the truth to draw away disciples after them." These historical perspectives highlight the enduring challenge posed by false prophets and the ongoing need for discernment within religious communities. Understanding the characteristics of false prophets is crucial for discernment. In addition to the biblical warnings, various passages provide insights into the traits of deceptive leaders. Jeremiah 23:16-17 describes false prophets in the context of their misleading messages: "This is what the Lord Almighty says: 'Do not listen to what the prophets are prophesying to you; they fill you with false hopes. They speak visions from their minds, not from the mouth of the Lord. They keep saying to those who despise me, "The Lord says: You will have peace." Moreover, to all who follow the stubbornness of their hearts, they say, "No harm will come to you.""

False prophets often speak messages catering to the people's desires, offering false assurances and promising peace without addressing the underlying issues of sin and disobedience. Additionally, **Matthew 24:24** warns of the deceptive nature of false prophets in the context of end-times prophecies: "For false messiahs and false prophets will appear and perform great signs and wonders to deceive, if possible, even the elect." Here, the danger lies in misleading words and the potential for deceptive miracles and signs that may accompany false prophets.

Discerning true revelations involves recognizing false prophets and embracing genuine encounters with the divine. In **1 Corinthians 14:29**, Paul guides the discernment of prophetic messages within the Christian community: "Two or three prophets should speak, and the others should weigh carefully what is said." This underscores the communal nature of discernment, suggesting that the responsibility to evaluate prophetic messages rests on the individual and the community.

The Apostle Paul also emphasizes the importance of aligning revelations with the established teachings of the faith. In **Galatians 1:8**, he strongly warns about deviations from the gospel: "But even if we or an angel from heaven should preach a gospel other than the one we preached to you, let them be under God's curse!" This implies that true revelations will always align with the core tenets of the faith and will not introduce doctrines that contradict the foundational truths of Scripture.

Additionally, **1 Thessalonians 5:19-22** provides practical guidance for discernment: "Do not quench the Spirit. Do not treat prophecies with contempt but test them all; hold on to what is good, reject every kind of evil." This encourages believers not to dismiss prophetic utterances outright but to test them against the principles of Scripture and the discernment of the Holy Spirit.

The Holy Spirit plays a central role in the discernment of revelations. Christ Jesus promises the Holy Spirit as a guide into all truth in St. **John 16:13;** "But when he, the Spirit of truth, comes, he will guide you into all the truth. He will not speak on his own; he will speak only what he hears and tell you what is yet to come." As the Spirit of truth, the Holy Spirit serves as believers' ultimate source of discernment, enabling them to recognize authentic revelations and discern falsehood.

Additionally, **1 John 2:20-21** emphasizes the indwelling of the Holy Spirit in believers as a source of discernment: "But you have an anointing from the Holy One, and all of you know the truth. I do not write to you because you do not know the truth but because you do know it and because no lie comes from the truth." The anointing of the Holy Spirit equips believers with a discerning spirit, allowing them to recognize and reject falsehood

While seeking revelations is a legitimate aspect of spiritual life, believers must approach this quest cautiously and humbly. While seeking revelations is a legitimate and enriching aspect of spiritual life, believers must approach this quest with caution and humility. The desire to hear from God and understand His will is noble, but it requires discernment to ensure that our perception aligns with the truth of Scripture and the character of God.

Pride or impatience can lead to misinterpretation or chasing after experiences rather than genuine spiritual growth. Believers must remain anchored in prayer, guided by the Word, and open to the counsel of mature Christians to avoid misleading by personal desires or external influences. Humility allows the Holy Spirit to work freely, ensuring that revelations are not self-serving but serve to glorify God and edify His people.

Reflection.

The Holy Spirit plays a central role in the discernment of revelations. Christ Jesus promises the Holy Spirit as a guide into all truth in St. **John 16:13;** "But when he, the Spirit of truth, comes, he will guide you into all the truth. He will not speak on his own; he will speak only what he hears and tell you what is yet to come

---

CHAPTER 7

PREACHER OF PERFORMER

The line between a preacher and a performer is subtle yet significant in religious discourse. While both may stand before an audience, the motives, methods, and impact can differ significantly. We must explore the distinctive characteristics that separate a genuine preacher from a mere performer. Drawing insights from scripture, historical examples, and practical considerations, we will delve into the essence of authentic preaching and the potential pitfalls associated with performance-oriented approaches.

The Divine Call to Preach: A divine calling is at the heart of authentic preaching. The Bible is replete with examples of individuals chosen and anointed by God to deliver His messages to the people. **Jeremiah 1:4-5** encapsulates the essence of a divine call to preach: "The word of the Lord came to me, saying, ' before I formed you in the womb, I knew you, before you were born, I set you apart; I appointed you as a prophet to the nations.'"

The call to preach is not a self-appointed role but a response to a divine call. In contrast, a performer's ambition is the motive, seeking applause and validation from the audience. A genuine preacher recognizes the gravity of the divine call and approaches the pulpit with reverence, humility, and accountability to God.

Preaching the Word of God. The authentic preaching anchored in the faithful proclamation of the enduring Word of God. **2 Timothy 4:2** encourages preachers with these words: "Preach the word; be prepared in season and out of season; correct, rebuke and encourage—with great patience and careful instruction." The emphasis is on the timeless importance of the Word of God in the preacher's message. A preacher, juxtapose to a performer, prioritizes the scriptural content of their message over personal charisma or entertainment value. The purpose is not to dazzle the audience with eloquence or theatrics but to convey the enduring truths of God's Word. In contrast, a performer may prioritize the audience's emotional response over fidelity to biblical truths.

The Focus on Transformation. Genuine preaching has a transformative impact on the lives of those who hear the message. **Romans 12:2** captures the essence of this transformative process: "Do not conform to the pattern of this world, but be transformed by the renewing of your mind. Then you can test and prove God's will his good, pleasing, and perfect will." A preacher seeks to lead individuals toward a deeper understanding of God's will, encouraging them to align their lives with divine principles. The goal is to evoke an emotional response and facilitate spiritual growth and maturity. In contrast, a performer may focus on eliciting applause or emotional reactions without necessarily fostering lasting change in the audience's lives.

Authenticity and Sincerity. One of the defining characteristics of a genuine preacher is authenticity. Authenticity entails a sincere and transparent connection between the preacher and the congregation. **2 Corinthians 4:2** underscores the importance of sincerity in preaching: "Rather, we renounce those secret and shameful ways; we do not use deception, nor do we distort the word of God. On the contrary, by setting forth the truth plainly, we commend ourselves to everyone's conscience in the sight of God." A preacher's authenticity reflects their commitment to truthfulness, humility, and vulnerability. Congregations are likelier to respond to a message delivered with genuine sincerity than to a performance laden with theatrics and artificiality.

Humility and Servant Leadership. Authentic preaching exemplifies humility and servant leadership. Jesus, the ultimate example of a servant leader, declared in **Matthew 20:28**. "Just as the Son of Man did not come to be served, but to serve, and to give his life as a ransom for many." A preacher, following in the footsteps of Christ, recognizes the role of humility and service in practical ministry. **Philippians 2:3-4** further emphasizes the importance of humility in leadership: "Do nothing out of selfish ambition or vain conceit. Rather, in humility, value others above yourselves, not looking to your interests but each of you to the interests of the others." A preacher's focus is serving the congregation's spiritual needs, not on self-promotion or seeking personal acclaim. In contrast, a performer aims for recognition, applause, and admiration. A preacher, grounded in humility and service, aligns himself with the biblical model of leadership exemplified by Jesus.

Anointing of the Holy Spirit. The effectiveness of authentic preaching aligns closely to the anointing of the Holy Spirit. **1 John 2:27** speaks to the role of the Holy Spirit in guiding and empowering believers: "As for you, the anointing you received from him remains in you, and you do not need anyone to teach you. But as his anointing teaches you about all things and as that anointing is real, not counterfeit just as it has taught you, remain in him." A preacher seeks the anointing of the Holy Spirit to illuminate the truth of God's Word, convict hearts, and bring about transformation. The reliance on the Holy Spirit distinguishes authentic preaching from a performance that relies solely on human skill or charisma.

Fruitfulness and Impact. Another significant aspect of authentic preaching is its fruitfulness and lasting impact. Jesus Christ, in the parable of the sower, illustrates the varying levels of receptivity to the Word of God [**St. Matthews 13:3-9**]. The seed that falls on good soil represents those who hear the message, understand it, and produce a fruitful crop. **Galatians 5:22-23** describes the fruits of the Spirit: "But the fruit of the Spirit is love, joy, peace, forbearance, kindness, goodness, faithfulness, gentleness, and self-control." We measure a preacher's impact not by the immediate emotional response of the audience but by the lasting fruits of transformed lives.

Accountability and Accountability. Authentic preachers operate within an accountability framework. **James 3:1** warns those who aspire to teach: "Not many of you should become teachers, my fellow believers because you know that we who teach God will judge more strictly." The recognition of the accountability before God for the words spoken from the pulpit adds a solemn dimension to the role of a preacher. Responsibility also involves submitting to the oversight and counsel of fellow believers. **Proverbs 11:14** states, "For lack of guidance a nation falls, but victory is won through many advisers." A preacher benefits from the guidance and correction of wise counselors who can help maintain doctrinal integrity and prevent the pitfalls of performance-driven ministry.

Avoiding the Traps of Performance. While focusing on performance style is performative elements are not inherently wrong, they can become problematic when they overshadow the substance of the message. Paul met Richard in the parking lot and waved him over. To his surprise, Richard discerned the same challenge. "We have put a lot of emphasis on the preaching ability of the pastor and not on our receiving revelations that will renew our mind," Richard said. Richard emphasized that maintaining the church's operation and growth has become one of many of the church's top priorities. This emphasis also requires significant financial contributions given regularly. Our church leaders aim to meet the church budget. Whereas this is important and foremost, the souls of the members and guests who enter the church each Sunday is crucial," Richard said.

Susan and Cathy spotted Richard and George standing in the parking lot. Susan and Cathy could sense the tone of their attitude by the seriousness of their demeanor. Their husbands' desire to know Christ and the power of His resurrection was the top priority. Susan and Cathy embraced their husbands and said, "God sees your heart."

"I understand, Cathy, but what do we do when God is silent," George said. "I believe God removes Himself from anyone who contradicts His will. Richard said we cannot judge our relationship with God based on the size of our church membership or material possessions. Is it possible that God is silent, and we revel in the idea of our Christianity and having fellowship with each other? We constantly talk about building projects and growing the church membership. How often do we talk about winning souls?"

"Perhaps God is silent," Richard said. Perhaps we have a form of godliness but deny the power thereof." "How do we know when God is not talking," Cathy asked. Richard folded his hands and sighed deeply. "Cathy, the silence of God can be unsettling, but it's something many of us experience at some point. Sometimes, it is not that God is not speaking; it is that we are not listening. We are so caught up in our routines or distracted by the noise of life that we miss His voice. Other times, it could be a matter of having a form of godliness but denying its power, similarly Paul warned in **2 Timothy.** If our faith becomes shallow or performative—focused on appearances rather than a genuine connection with God—we might find it harder to sense His presence or discern His guidance. His silence could be His way of calling us to examine our hearts, repent, and seek Him more earnestly."

Cathy leaned forward, her brow furrowed. "But how do we know when it's God not talking and not just us missing Him?" she asked. Richard nodded thoughtfully. "That's a good question. When God seems silent, we should first reflect on our relationship with Him. Are we spending time in His Word? Are we praying sincerely or just going through the motions? Sometimes, God uses silence to grow our faith, teaching us to trust Him even when we do not hear Him. Other times, His silence might be a response to unrepented sin or a hardened heart. It is essential to approach Him with humility, asking, 'Lord, is there anything in me that's blocking your voice?' And even in the silence, we can hold onto His promises, knowing that He is always with us, even when we can't feel or hear Him."

CHAPTER 8

WHEN GOD IS SILENT

Are there moments when God is not talking? The moments when God seems silent is a profound and perplexing aspect of the spiritual journey. The perceived absence of divine communication can evoke emotions, from confusion and doubt to longing and spiritual thirst. We must know that habitual sin separates us from God. We are all sinners saved by the grace of God. However, we can also anchor our souls to habitual sins that God hates unknowingly. We see ourselves as devout Christians. However, God considers our behavior as an abomination **[Proverbs 6:16-18]**. Consequently, God becomes silent. Then, the voices we hear or the knowledge we attain did not come from God. We have only sought to establish our righteousness **[Romans 10:3]. W**e strive to unravel the mysteries of divine silence and offer guidance for those navigating the spiritual wilderness.

God's silence does not necessarily indicate indifference or abandonment. There are instances in scripture where God's silence serves a purpose beyond immediate comprehension.

The theological exploration of divine silence encompasses a nuanced understanding of God's character and His ways. The Bible affirms the sovereignty of God, acknowledging that His thoughts are higher than our thoughts and His ways beyond our understanding **[Isaiah 55:8-9]**. This acknowledgment lays the foundation for comprehending the mysteries of God's silence. God's silence does not necessarily indicate indifference or abandonment. There are instances in scripture where God's silence serves a purpose beyond immediate comprehension. **Habakkuk 1:13** captures this tension: "Your eyes are too pure to look on evil; you cannot tolerate the idea of wrong doing." Sometimes, God's silence may invite introspection, repentance, or a deeper reliance on faith. The Bible emphasizes God's unchanging nature. Hebrews 13:8 declares, "Jesus Christ is the same yesterday and today and forever." This fundamental truth anchors us in seasons of divine silence, assuring us that God's character remains constant even when His voice is not audible.

Exploring the scriptural narratives of divine silence provides insights into how individuals in the Bible navigated periods of apparent quietness from God. The stories of biblical figures such as Job, Elijah, and David offer glimpses into the complexities of divine silence and the subsequent revelations of God's purposes.

1. **Job's Lament**: The narrative of Job is a poignant exploration of suffering, questioning, and divine silence. In the face of overwhelming adversity, Job lamented, "If only I knew where to find him; if only I could go to his dwelling! I would state my case before him and fill my mouth with arguments" **[Job 23:3-4]**.
2. **Elijah's Wilderness Experience**: The Prophet Elijah's journey through the wilderness exemplifies by divine silence. After experiencing a remarkable victory against the prophets

of Baal, Elijah faced the threat of Queen Jezebel, prompting him to flee to the wilderness in despair **[1 Kings 19:1-18]**.

3. **David's Psalms of Lament**: The Psalms, attributed mainly to King David, resonate with the raw emotions of lament, questioning, and a sense of divine absence **[Psalm 13:1-2]** captures the essence of David's cry: "How long, Lord? Will you forget me forever? How long will you hide your face from me? How long must I wrestle with my thoughts and have sorrow in my heart daily?"

Beyond the theological realm, God's silence has psychological and emotional implications for individuals traversing the spiritual wilderness. Understanding these dimensions can provide a holistic perspective on the human experience of divine silence.

The experience of God's silence may manifest as a spiritual dryness, a sense of desolation, or a feeling of abandonment. This arid spiritual landscape can lead to a profound sense of emptiness, causing individuals to question the authenticity of their faith.

Divine silence can precipitate a crisis of faith characterized by doubt, questioning, and a sense of spiritual disorientation. In these moments, individuals may grapple with the foundational tenets of their belief system, questioning the reality of God's existence or the validity of their faith. God's silence often intensifies the longing for assurance and tangible signs of His presence. The desire for a clear word from God, a miraculous intervention, or an authentic experience heightens during periods of silence. Amid the spiritual wilderness, practical strategies can serve as guiding lights for individuals seeking to navigate God's silence with resilience, faith, and trust. These strategies encompass both individual and communal approaches to spiritual well-being.

Embracing stillness amid divine silence creates space for heightened awareness and receptivity. Practices such as contemplative prayer, meditation, and mindfulness can foster a spirit of peace that allows individuals to attune their hearts to God's subtle whispers.

Reflection.

Does your faith in Christ Jesus reside on the surface, or does it penetrate your heart and change you from the inside out? Doing good does not make us good. God wants us to do well, but He is more interested in following His righteousness **[St. Matthews 6:33]**. Only those who have a sincere relationship with our Heavenly Father can truly know Him. Ask the Lord to lead you into a faith based on a deeper revelation based on His Word. Today is a great day to start.

CHAPTER 9

FLAWED TRUTHS

The Bible has been the subject of diverse interpretations throughout history. While many find profound inspiration and guidance in its pages, discussions about perceived flawed truths arise when individuals or groups grapple with specific passages, doctrines, or cultural contexts. The fundamental problem is that one can take the text literally without understanding the context. We must examine biblical interpretation by delving into theological, historical, and ethical dimensions. These flawed truths are under-penned by wrongful hermeneutics.

One of biblical interpretation's perennial debates revolves around understanding specific passages literally or allegorically. This distinction is the accounts of creation, miracles, and apocalyptic visions. The Bible reflects the cultural contexts in which the authors wrote. We must consider some passages' interpretations with ethical considerations. Cultural norms, moral teachings, and the treatment of certain groups are areas where differing interpretations may arise.

Theological doctrines and interpretations of critical concepts vary among Christian denominations, leading to differences in understanding fundamental truths. The transmission and translation of the Bible over centuries have led to textual variants and manuscript differences. Scholars use textual criticism to understand these variants' impact on specific passages' reliability.

Perceived flawed truths in biblical interpretation often arise from the complex interplay of cultural, historical, theological, and ethical considerations. As believers, our engagement in discussions about these complexities is not just crucial, but it is the very heart of the matter. Our respectful approach to differing interpretations and recognition of the diverse perspectives within the broader tapestry of religious dialogue are what make this ongoing exploration of perceived flaws so significant. Our active participation contributes to a deeper understanding of the intricate nature of biblical interpretation and the constant quest for spiritual truth.

George and Richard scheduled a meeting with Pastor Howell. Both were anxious because they were confused about specific doctrines and did not want to disrespect their pastor. However, there were awash of truths that confused them. All four George, Susan, Richard, and Cathy—took copious notes each Sunday. After reviewing those notes over the last few weeks, they realized they needed Rhema rather than a feel-good card. They required the allure God offered.

As usual, Pastor Howell showed superb hospitality. He was a loving pastor, a good family man, and spent much time and energy in the community. Pastor Howell was the pastor of Redeeming Faith for over 25 years. In addition, he pastored two other churches for 40 years in pastoral ministry. It was clear to George that Pastor Howell understood how to reach people. George's question resided in the fact that he had plateaued in his spiritual walk. Indeed, he could not lay all of this responsibility on Pastor Howell. He was responsible for his spiritual growth through prayer time and studying God's word. He needed Pastor Howell to help him understand some of his recent biblical truths. He wanted to be accurate in his revelation and not spread false doctrine.

"Thank you for scheduling this time with us, Pastor. We can imagine how busy you are," George said. Pastor Howell, with his usual warmth, embraced both George and Richard. His smile and show of concern, support, and love had a disarming effect on everyone. "No, anytime, George. Both of your families are important to me and our church; how can I help you and Richard today," Pastor Howell replied, showing his understanding and empathy. George and Richard began to review a list of biblical truths. They discovered these truths, seeking to ensure they did not misunderstand or embrace a false belief. Their determination was not to lead their families into error.

Richard saw George struggling and took the reins in the discussion. "Pastor Howell, we have a list of what we believe are biblical truths. I want to give you the list and discuss each one. Our concern is that we heard these spiritual topics preached and taught by many television evangelists, including you, Pastor Howell. "With all due respect, Pastor Howell, the truths we heard and believed have flaws based on reading a text. However, we examined the context; the teaching may have missed the mark," Richard said. Richard gave the list of what he considered "flawed truths" and explained the recent revelations he and George uncovered. Richard said, "Please be patient as I list the ten flawed truths. We may have confused ourselves and completely made a big error, but we want to know what's true and TRUTH," Richard added. He lists includes the following.

1. Text versus context when studying scriptures
2. What do plead the blood and cover in the blood mean?
3. Why do we close our prayers in the name of Jesus, and what does that mean?
4. Who is The Holy Spirit?
5. And there is MORE.

Pastor Howell sat in amazement. At that moment, he realized that he based most of his beliefs on what his pastor and other spiritual leaders taught him. He never studied the Bible from the perspective of finding the TRUTH. He studied the Bible to confirm and reaffirm what he believed. Pastor Howell told Richard, "I just received an understanding from our discussion and need some time to process the discussion." Pastor Howell's response amazed George. George firmly believed that the Holy Spirit appointed him this assignment. This assignment was to reveal the God of the Bible and not the God of the church. As he and Richard left Pastor Howell's office, he came to the following conclusions.

INTERPRETING THE BIBLE. This is a crucial task, and there are several common pitfalls to avoid. Our effort is discipleship, not just becoming a Christian. We must ignore traditions, customs, and doctrines. We must avoid the critical pitfalls in our effort to discover the truth of the Bible, God's word.

The writers of the Old and New Testaments wrote in Hebrew, Aramaic, and Koine Greek. As the Word of God expanded, Jews translated portions of the Bible into Koine Greek. The Greeks translated the Hebrew texts into Greek and produced a Greek version of the Bible in 1638. Unfortunately, many Bible scholars struggle with the Hebrew and Aramaic languages and choose to use the Greek translation. The Greek context is entirely different from the Hebrew and Aramaic context. This difference is where the confusion begins. We assumed that Greeks wrote the Word of God in the Old Testament. We have no evidence of this statement. One truth is that God does not change **[Malachi 3:6]**. There is evidence that, on occasions, the Apostle Paul was speaking in Aramaic. The Apostle Paul often spoke in Aramaic. **In Acts 22:1-2**, Paul says the following:

> "**Men, brethren, and fathers hear ye my defense which I make now unto you. (And when they heard that he spoke in the Hebrew tongue to them, they kept the more silence: and he saith,)³ I am certainly a man who is a Jew, born in Tarsus, a city in Cilicia, yet brought up in this city at the feet of Gamaliel, and taught according to the perfect manner of the law of the fathers, and was zealous toward God, as ye all are this day.**"

The Bible consists of sixty-six books written for revelation. Inspired by God, each human author wrote in a specific culture and addressed a particular audience at a specific time. Thus, we best understand what they communicated within the context in which they wrote. Hence, the process of inductive Bible study.

ONE VALID INTERPRETATION: While believers may differ on difficult passages, every passage has only one valid, correct interpretation. God's Word is objective truth, and it is essential to approach it carefully and reverently **[2 Timothy 3:16-17, Colossians 2:8]**. If something is objective, it corresponds with reality. Objective truth is actual for everyone, whether everyone agrees with it or not. *Objective* is the opposite of *subjective*. If someone says, "The 1966 Ford Mustang is the coolest car ever made," he is making a subjective statement. It is simply the opinion of one person. There is no way to measure that statement against reality. We cannot honestly evaluate the statement apart from other people's views. Others will either support or oppose the statement, depending solely on their equally subjective views. It is impossible to say that a subjective statement is true in any meaningful sense; however, in modern parlance, someone might say, "It is MY truth," which introduces a brand-new spin on subjectivism. At one time, "my truth" more accurately labeled "my opinion."

An objective statement is factual; it has a definite correspondence to reality, independent of anyone's feelings or biases. If someone says, "I own a 1966 Ford Mustang," he makes an objective statement. If that person owns such a car, then the statement is true. The statement is false if a person does not own such a car. The truth or falsehood of the claim does not depend upon subjective opinion.

More often, religion usually attacks the very concept of objective truth. Things deemed as objective by certain religions are subjective. For instance, the simple statement "God exists" was, in the past, recognized as an objective statement. People might agree or disagree, but everyone considered it an objective statement regarding external reality. Most people agreed with the statement, but even atheists who disagreed treated it objectively—the statement was either true or false.

In summary, facts and opinions are different. Objective truth is the opposite of (subjective) opinion. People may argue over whether a particular statement is objective or subjective. If it is objective, they may say whether it is true. However, no matter what, it is impossible to escape the fact that objective truth does exist. At one time, the job of the Christian was to demonstrate the truthfulness of the biblical claims. Now, the preacher's assignment is more difficult because, before discussing the truth of the Bible, the Christian must often convince the listener that truth exists, especially touching religious claims.

Man tends to allow religion to creep into their understanding of God's word. We must understand that the LORD did not create religion. Man created religion for many reasons, but religion is an interpretation of who God is. Religion focuses on church doctrine, and the methods of how we conduct church. Man's word is far from the truth. It seems fitting to man, but it is an error to God. The most challenging task of finding truth is to lay aside our religion, which is man's interpretation of God, by seeking the truth of the word of God in context.

Proverbs 14:12 cautions us that sometimes, what seems like a wise and reasonable path may ultimately lead to negative consequences. Human reasoning and desires can be misleading. We must behave cautiously to avoid following paths that appear right but ultimately result in harm. It serves as a reminder to seek wisdom, listen to God's Word, and avoid relying solely on our understanding.

God's Word: It is factual, pure, genuine, and reality. God cannot lie, and His Word reflects His character. Many believers search for a spiritual "nugget" and miss the opportunity to know God. The Bible explains the character of God and his sovereignty. **St. Matthews 6:33** clearly instructs us to seek the Kingdom of God and His righteousness first. His Kingdom is his authority, power, and rule. His righteousness is His way of doing things. These two parts explain the unchangeable character of God.

Man's Word: Flawed, sometimes genuine, sometimes not. Our experiences and limitations affect our ability to convey the ultimate truth. Men argue about meaning points like what day to worship or whose name we baptize in. The central theme of God's creative work is in **St. John 3:16**. When we mediate and understand the magnitude of God's love, we seek to find His character and ways of doing things.

Hermeneutics: The science of interpretation (hermeneutics) seeks to understand the writer's original intent. We aim to grasp the human writer's understanding and God's deeper intent. Hermeneutics is critical to understanding the scripture. However, hermeneutics focuses on the context of scripture instead of the literal scripture of focus. Hermeneutics studies the scripture around and the scripture of focus to understand the proper interpretation. Some scriptures where the context is missed are the following.

- **St. Luke 6:38** is not about giving money. This scripture is about giving grace and love.
- **1 Corinthians 16:2.** This scripture is about giving to missions rather than the tithe and offerings God expects.

Law of Non-Contradiction: The bible will not contradict itself because it is God's word, and God is faithful. We see the Bible as the infallible word of God **[2 Timothy 3:16-17].**

Biblical interpretation requires humility, prayer, and reliance on the Holy Spirit to guide us into all truth. We must approach the Bible with the expectation that God wants to reveal Himself to us.

George explained to Richard the next steps. "We must take time to study the flawed truths we have been taught. I do not believe many preachers/teachers intend to teach us a non-truth. But, we must study so we can rightly divide the word of truth for our next assignment," George said. Richard nodded his head in agreement.

Richard thought how incredible this experience was for him and his family. God had allowed him to mature spiritually. "Let's meet Sunday night, George, and work on ten (10) flawed truths," Richard said. George replied, "You got it, Richard. Let us meet on Sunday at 5:00 PM. We will take whatever time it takes to understand these flawed truths."

As George drove back home, he realized that the LORD was leading him on a journey of spiritual development for something greater. The LORD would reveal the "greater" in due season. While he waited, George's determination was undeniable.

FLAWED TRUTH #1

Text versus Context in Studying the Scriptures.

Many biblical errors occur because of our lack of understanding of two main principles in understanding God's word, the Bible. Many people read scripture and interpret its meaning or attempt to understand it from their point of reference. This is flawed because we should not use the Bible to prove or reaffirm our beliefs. The Bible is not a collection of thoughts; it is a book of revelations on who God is that provides instructions on what God expects or His purpose for us. When we fall short of looking at the totality of the instruction, we lose the true essence of God and His instructions for our lives.

When studying the Bible, we must understand that there are two crucial elements to gain insight into what the LORD is saying. These two essential elements are the text and context. Let us examine the definitions for both of these words

- *Text* – the parts of something written or spoken that include a word or passage of scripture.
- *Context*—the parts of something written or spoken that immediately precede and follow a word or passage of scripture that clarifies its meaning and associated reference scriptures. Understand the context is when Rhema occurs. Rhema can only happen through study [2 Timothy 2:15-18]. This type of study provides the revelation.

The Apostle Paul did not tell us to use the logos to receive revelation of the word of God. His instruction was to Rhema the word of God [2 Timothy 2:15]. The reason for the study is to accomplish the following:

We must present ourselves in a way that will allow us to receive God's approval.

1. A workman tested by trial who has no reason to be ashamed.
2. A workman who accurately handles and skillfully teaches the word of truth.
3. A workman that avoids all irreverent babble and godless chatter [with its profane, empty words], for it will lead to further ungodliness.

Consequently, to receive the revelations of God's word or a Rhema word, we must study the pretext and post texts to understand the context or revelation.

Let us review an example to understand this principle of study.

EXAMPLE#1

Christ Jesus instructed about "Truth" [**St. John 8:28 - 29**].

PRETEXT

- He reaffirms His identity [**St. John 8:25**]
- He confirms that the Father is TRUTH [**St. John 8:26**].
- His death and resurrection will confirm His identity [**St. John 8:28-29**]
- He speaks about the requirements of discipleship, and His disciples know the truth [**St. John 8:31**].

The pretext explains a part of a conversation between Jesus and a group of Jews questioning him. Here is the passage: "So Jesus said, 'When you have lifted the Son of Man, then you will know that I am he and do nothing on my own but speak just what the Father has taught me. The one who sent me is with me; he has not left me alone, for I always do what pleases him.' Even as he spoke, many believed in him."

To the Jews who had believed him, Jesus said, 'If you hold to my teaching, you are my disciples. Then you will know the truth, and the truth will set you free.'" In this passage, Jesus foreshadows his crucifixion ("When you have lifted the Son of Man") and emphasizes the connection between him and God the Father. He also speaks about the importance of holding to his teaching to be his disciples and the liberating power of knowing the truth. In this context, the truth is likely referring to the spiritual truth that Jesus brings, which leads to freedom from sin and a deeper understanding of God's plan for salvation.

This verse is part of a larger discourse that Jesus had with some Jews who did not believe in him. He was trying to explain to them his identity and his relationship with God the Father. He used the metaphor of "lifting" the Son of Man to refer to his crucifixion and resurrection, which would reveal his true nature as the Messiah and the Son of God. He also claimed that he was not acting on his authority but only doing and saying what God the Father instructed him to do.

Here, Jesus affirmed that God the Father was always with and supported him in His mission. He also stated that His goal was to please God the Father by obeying His will. Because of His words, many of the Jews who heard Him became His followers. Here, Jesus invited those who believed in Him to remain faithful to His teachings and to follow Him as His disciples. He promised them they would know the truth, the revelation of God's love and grace through Him. He also assured them that the truth would set them free from the penalty of sin and death.

POST TEXT

To further understand St. John 8:28-30, we must study the scripture following our text. St. **John 8:31-32** brings further clarity. In these verses, we encounter a profound discourse by Jesus that delves into the essence of truth and freedom. This passage resonates deeply with seekers of spiritual wisdom across centuries, offering insights that transcend the boundaries of time and culture. The verses read:

"31 So Jesus said to the Jews who had believed him, 'If you abide in my word, you are truly my disciples, 32 and you will know the truth, and the truth will set you free.'" (John 8:31-32 ESV)

This passage encapsulates Jesus Christ's fundamental teachings regarding the transformative power of truth and the liberating nature of genuine discipleship. In John 8, Jesus finds himself engaged in a heated dialogue with a group of Jews who professed belief in him. However, their understanding of discipleship was superficial, lacking genuine commitment and adherence to his teachings.

The Context.

Jesus begins by outlining the prerequisite for authentic discipleship: abiding in his word. This goes beyond mere intellectual acceptance or occasional adherence to his teachings. Abiding, in his words, implies a deep, intimate relationship characterized by obedience, trust, and continuous learning. It is a commitment of the heart, mind, and soul to the principles and truths embodied in Jesus's words.

Jesus declares that those who abide in his word will "know the truth." Here, truth transcends mere factual knowledge or intellectual understanding. It encompasses a profound spiritual enlightenment—a transformative realization of the ultimate reality and divine purpose underlying existence. This truth is not a static concept but a dynamic, living reality that unfolds progressively as one walks the path of discipleship.

Central to Jesus' message is the assertion that the truth will "make you free." This liberation is twofold: freedom from the bondage of sin and falsehood and freedom to live in alignment with God's will and purpose. It liberates individuals from the shackles of ignorance, delusion, and spiritual captivity, empowering them to experience the fullness of life and communion with the Divine.

Jesus presents discipleship as the pathway to freedom. True discipleship entails not only belief but also active participation in the transformative journey of spiritual growth and realization. Spiritual growth involves surrendering one's will to the divine will, embracing the teachings of Jesus, and embodying His love, compassion, and righteousness in daily life.

Implications for contemporary life.

The timeless wisdom in **John 8:31-32** holds profound implications for contemporary individuals and societies. Pursuing truth and freedom remains an urgent imperative in an age characterized by moral relativism, spiritual disillusionment, and existential uncertainty. **John 8:31-32** is a beacon of spiritual enlightenment and ethical guidance, inviting humanity to embark on a transformative journey of truth seeking and discipleship. It calls us to transcend the limitations of egoism consciousness and awaken to the liberating power of divine truth. May we heed Jesus' invitation, abide by His word, and experience the boundless freedom that comes from knowing and embracing the truth.

CONTEXT

Jesus is Christ, the Messiah, the Father in the flesh **[St. John 1:14]** dwelt among us to reveal God's plan. God desired to free us from the bondage and penalty of sin. Our choices will cause us to disobey God's laws and lead us to sin **[Romans 3:23]**. However, Christ reveals the truth of God's intention and shows us that He is our example of living for God in a world entirely of sin **[St. John 14:9]**. God loved us so much that He revealed this truth to remove the fear and help us love and know God through Jesus Christ **[St. John 3:16]**.

The textual scripture holds profound significance within the broader context of the Gospel of John and the theological themes it encapsulates. These verses, often called the discourse on truth and freedom, provide insight into the teachings of Jesus Christ and the implications for human understanding and salvation. **St. John 8:28-32** occurs within the broader narrative of Jesus' ministry and teachings. In this passage, Jesus speaks to a crowd, declaring Himself as the Son of God and emphasizing the necessity of believing in Him for true freedom. The context of **St. John 8:28-30** is about TOTAL FREEDOM. This declaration of divine identity is central to the Gospel of John's overarching theme of Christology, which focuses on the nature and significance of Jesus as the Word made flesh **[St. John 1:14]**.

Several scriptures within the New Testament complement and expand upon the themes presented in St. John 8:28-30. For instance, in **John 14:6**, Jesus declares, "I am the way and the truth and the life. No one comes to the Father except through me." This statement reinforces the exclusivity of Christ as the path to salvation and underscores the intimate connection between truth, life, and relationship with God. This context explains TOTAL FREEDOM.

Furthermore, the concept of freedom articulated in **St. John 8:28-30** finds resonance in other New Testament writings. In **Galatians 5:1**, the apostle Paul writes, "It is for freedom that Christ has set us free. Stand firm, then, and do not let yourselves be burdened again by a yoke of slavery." Here, Paul emphasizes the liberating power of Christ's sacrifice, which liberates believers from the bondage of sin and legalistic observance.

Interpreting **St. John 8:28-30** in light of its contexts enables a deeper understanding of its relevance for contemporary Christian life. The passage challenges believers to reflect on the nature of truth and the implications of discipleship in pursuing spiritual freedom. It calls for a radical commitment to Christ as the embodiment of truth and the source of authentic liberation.

Moreover, the message of **St. John 8:28-30** invites believers to examine their understanding of truth and freedom amid contemporary challenges and complexities. In a world marked by relativism, skepticism, and moral ambiguity, the call to abide in Christ's truth and experience GENIUNE FREEDOM takes on renewed significance. **St. John 8:28-30** and related scriptures offer profound insights into truth, freedom, and discipleship within the Christian faith. We gain a deeper appreciation for their enduring relevance and transformative power by situating these verses within the appropriate contexts. As believers engage with these teachings, they must embrace the truth of Christ and experience the liberating freedom found in Him.

The truth will make you free from the bondage of sin [St. John 8:31-32]. The truth will not make us free from sinning, but rather make us true from the bondage of sin [St. John 8:34]. Therefore, we are free to make a choice [St. John 8:35, 36].

George and Richard arrived and opened their Bibles. "Where do we start," Richard asked. Let us examine the ten flaw truths we discussed with Pastor Howell.

Things to Think About. In the space below, write your spiritual thoughts and the revelation from this flawed truth:

What I did not know.

_____

_____

_____

What I learned.

_____

_____

_____

What I will do with what I learned.

_____

_____

_____

FLAWED TRUTH #2

Plead the Blood and Covered in the Blood.

"Pleading the blood of Jesus" is a phrase often used in Christian religious contexts, particularly within certain charismatic and Pentecostal traditions. It is believed that Christians receive it as a symbolic and metaphorical expression rather than a literal action. The concept is rooted in the belief that the blood of Jesus, shed on the cross according to Christian doctrine, has spiritual significance and power. Christians who use this phrase typically see the blood of Jesus as a symbol of atonement, redemption, and protection. Unfortunately, this belief is a flawed truth. In the Bible, no Prophet or Apostle says to plead the blood or that we are covered in the blood.

When someone says they are "pleading the blood of Jesus," they are in error. They attempt to invoke the spiritual benefits of Jesus' sacrifice for forgiveness of sins, protection from harm, and deliverance from evil. They use this expression to express faith in the transformative and protective power of Jesus' sacrifice. However, this is a flawed truth.

The phrase **"covered by the blood of Jesus"** is another expression within certain Christian traditions, often associated with protection, redemption, and salvation. It is a metaphorical concept rooted in Christian theology. Whereas the blood explains God's grace and mercy toward us, it does not explain the result of God's redemption. Christ paid for our sins through His death. However, His death did not cover us in His blood.

In Christian belief, the shedding of Jesus' blood on the cross is a sacrifice that atones for humanity's sins. The blood is symbolic of redemption and forgiveness. When someone says they are "covered by the blood of Jesus," they are expressing the belief that the blood protects and cleanses from sin through faith in Jesus and his sacrifice. This is a flawed truth. **1 John 1:9** gives us the requirement for the forgiveness and cleansing of our unrighteousness.

God's remedy for our sin is the death of Christ Jesus. We must understand how God established His covenants with us. He gave us the Old Testament and the New Testament. The word "Testament" means "Contract." We benefit from the Old and New Testaments. These contracts are God's irreversible and irrevocable promises to us.

We must example the nature of the contracts.

- Why the new contract? **[Hebrews 9:23]**.
- The truth about God's new contract **[Hebrews 9:11-28]**.
- The reason for God's new contract **[Hebrews 9:16-18]**.

We must examine the true meaning of Christ shedding His blood. Shedding blood is how God established the cost of redemption **[Hebrews 9:22]**. We must understand what redemption means.

Redemption – Hebrew = ***Ga'al*** =" buy back". Therefore, God paid the price for our sins by shedding the blood of his "begotten" son. Therefore, we do not die immediately when we sin because of God's new will.

IN GOD'S OLD WILL. God expected the shedding of the blood of living creatures as a redemption for sin **[Hebrews 9:19-21]**. God expected a life for a life – that is the reason for the shedding of blood. Consequently, this will shed a living creature's blood each time man sinned.

IN GOD'S NEW COVENANT NEW WILL. God's new covenant is ETERNAL REDEMPTION {Hebrews 9:15].

- Eternal means it has no beginning or end.

Therefore, the shedding of blood means Christ died for us. Christ's death settles our sins with God. Our role is a confession, but Christ's death provided redemption. Therefore, the expression shedding of blood simply means the death of a life for a life. **Hebrews 9:23-25** provides the clarity.

[23] It was then necessary for the copies of the heavenly things to be purified with these sacrifices. Still, the heavenly things themselves with better sacrifices than these. [24] For Christ did not enter a sanctuary made with human hands that was only a copy of the true one; he entered heaven itself, now to appear for us in God's presence. [25] Nor did he enter heaven to offer himself again and again, the way the high priest enters the Most Holy Place every year with blood that is not his own [Hebrews 9:23-25].

Christ died to take away the penalty for our sins. We are not covered by the blood or have to plead the blood. God's eternal redemption through Christ remedied this sin problem. **Hebrews 9:28** gives us the revelation.

"[28] so Christ was sacrificed once to take away the sins of many; and he will appear a second time, not to bear sin, but to bring salvation to those waiting for him [Hebrews 9:28]."

God does not require us to plead the blood. We do not have to beg God to save us. We believe and confess, and He forgives our sins and cleanses us from all unrighteousness **[I John 1:9]**. The biblical truth is that Christ Jesus' blood redeemed us by dying in our place to remove us from the penalty of sin so that we could reign with God in eternity.

Things to Think About. In the space below, write your spiritual thoughts and the revelation from this flawed truth:

_____

_____

_____

_____

_____

_____

FLAWED TRUTH #3

What does in the name of Jesus mean?

Prayers across all Christian denominations close prayers with the expression "in the name of Jesus." Many take this expression out of context for a millennium. Satan attempts to minimize the power given to us by a living Savior. By declaring "in His name" out of context, we hand it to Jesus Christ, who will handle it. WRONG. What is the power of a name?

Therefore, names matter. A name can connect us to our identity and individuality and carry power, responsibility, and blessings to another powerful, reputable, and immutable source. Nowhere in scripture does it say by the name of Jesus, but rather in the name of Christ Jesus **[Acts 3:6]**. We were made whole and holy by calling **on the name** of the Lord Jesus Christ **[I Corinthians 16:11]**.

It is essential to understand 1 Corinthians 16:11's written context to grasp its significance. The apostle Paul addressed a community grappling with internal divisions, moral challenges, and doctrinal controversies. He offered a series of exhortations to foster spiritual maturity, unity, and steadfastness in the face of adversity.

Be Watchful.

The opening injunction, "Be watchful," calls to vigilance and spiritual awareness. It urges believers to remain alert to the subtle influences of temptation, deception, and spiritual warfare that threaten to undermine their faith and integrity. In a world marked by moral ambiguity and spiritual peril, this admonition reminds us of the importance of maintaining a vigilant posture, guarding our hearts and minds against the allure of sin and falsehood.

Stand Firm in the Faith.

The second appeal, "Stand firm in the faith," underscores the importance of unwavering commitment to the foundational truths of the Christian faith. It calls believers to anchor themselves securely in the bedrock of God's Word, refusing to be swayed by the shifting tides of cultural relativism, skepticism, or doctrinal compromise. In an age of intellectual skepticism and moral relativism, this call to steadfastness is a bulwark against the erosion of biblical truth and the dilution of authentic Christian witness.

Act like Men.

The phrase "act like men" many interpret and debated by scholars and theologians. While traditionally understood as a call to courage, strength, and maturity, it is crucial to recognize that the underlying Greek word ***"andrizomai"*** can also mean as "be courageous" or "be strong." Thus, this exhortation encompasses both genders and speaks to the universal need for courage and fortitude in adversity. It summons believers to embrace a spirit of boldness, resilience, and moral courage as they navigate the challenges of life and ministry.

Be Strong:

The final injunction, "Be strong," reinforces the preceding exhortations and encapsulates the overarching theme of fortitude and resilience. It reminds believers that their strength does not originate from human effort or worldly prowess but derives from their union with the empowering presence of the Holy Spirit. It is a summons to draw upon the inexhaustible reservoir of divine grace and strength made available to them through faith in Christ.

The wisdom encapsulated in **1 Corinthians 16:11** holds profound implications for contemporary believers navigating the complexities of life in the twenty-first century. In an era marked by rapid social change, moral upheaval, and spiritual warfare, the call to vigilance, steadfastness, courage, and strength resonates with renewed urgency and relevance.

1 Corinthians 16:11 stands as a beacon of spiritual wisdom and moral guidance, offering timeless counsel to believers seeking to navigate the vicissitudes of life with diligence and discernment. It beckons us to embrace a posture of spiritual vigilance, unwavering faith, moral courage, and divine strength as we journey through the complexities of the human experience. May we heed the Apostle Paul's exhortation, drawing inspiration and empowerment from Christ's indwelling presence and the gospel's transformative power?

Paul **[Philippians 2:9-11]** expresses the power of His name. However, we must see ourselves as Christ's Ambassadors; we are Ambassadors for Christ **[2 Corinthians 5:20]**. What is an Ambassador? A country sends an accredited diplomat as its official representative to a foreign country. As Ambassadors, we understand that we are Christ's earthly representative and go by the authority of His name and on Christ's behalf.

Therefore, the in name of means "by the authority and power given to us" by Christ Jesus. **Amen**

Things to Think About. In the space below, write your spiritual thoughts and the revelation from this flawed truth:

_____

_____

_____

_____

_____

FLAWED TRUTH #4

Predestination and Election.

Predestination and election are theological concepts within Christian doctrine that primarily come from the perspective of certain branches of Reformed theology, particularly associated with John Calvin's teachings. These concepts address questions about God's sovereignty, human free will, and salvation.

Predestination is the belief that God, before the creation of the world, chose specific individuals to be saved or damned. This choice does not comprehend action on the part of the individual but is solely according to God's sovereign will. Supporters of the doctrine often point to passages in the Bible, such as **Ephesians 1:4-5**, which instructs us that God chose believers in Christ before the foundation of the world.

The principle of Election relates to predestination. It refers to God's choosing of individuals for salvation. Those who are "elect" are the ones God has chosen to receive His grace and salvation. Biblical references to the election can be found in various passages, including **Romans 8:29-30,** which speaks of those God foreknew, predestined, and called.

It is important to note that not all Christian denominations or theological traditions similarly accept predestination and election doctrines. Theologians and denominations within the broader Christian spectrum have different views on the interplay between God's sovereignty and human free will in the process of salvation. The doctrine of predestination and election contradicts **Romans 1:9**. This doctrine presupposes that God knows who will be saved regardless of our human effort to align ourselves with His will and enter His kingdom **[St. Matthews 6:33]**.

Let us examine **Romans 8:29 (KJV):** "For whom he did foreknow, he also predestinate to be conformed to the image of his Son, that he might be the firstborn among many brethren."

Many people and some theologians take Paul's theology about predestination and election out of context. The FLAWED TRUTH is that God has already decided who is going to heaven and hell. Therefore, why did the LORD give us a "CHOICE?" The thought that God has favorites is WRONG **[Romans 2:11]**.

Look at **St. John 3:16. God so loved the World**. The requirement is to believe in His Son and have everlasting life {Become a Son of God].

- Believe – Hebrew – *Aman* – Firm obedience

Let us read the scripture as it is written in Hebrew: God so loves the world that He gave His only begotten [brought forth] Son, that whoever would **OBEY** Him shall have everlasting life. God's election: His method for redemption and restoring man to the position He gave Adam. God's election: the chosen people, or people of God, who are faithful to their divine call of salvation. Paul explains this foreknowing,

"For whom He did foreknow, He also predestinate to be conformed to the image of His Son." Whom did He foreknow? **[St. John 1:1-2, 14].** Christ is the firstborn of the Sons of God through His death, burial, and resurrection **[Romans 8:28].** This scripture is talking about Christ and not us. God foreknows Christ as the remedy for sin.

Paul says we should be like our elder brother, the Son of God**.** We proudly wear the name "Christian," which God never gave us. The men of Antioch mocked Jesus' disciples and gave that name to Christ's disciples, and we have worn it ever since **[Acts 11:26].** The name Christian minimizes our calling to God. The Apostle Paul instructs us that we are called to be Saints **[Romans 1:7].** The Aramaic meaning of the name Saint is *"gaddish"* and means "holy" or "set apart."

God wants Sons and not labels (neutral tense). Paul expresses God's desire in the following points. We are to be as follows:

- Conformed into the image of Christ **[2 Corinthians 3:18], AND**
- The whole earth travelieth wait for the manifestation of the Sons of God **[Romans 8:19].**

Therefore, the truth of the scripture is that God's will is that we all transform into the image of Christ. He desires us all to have the privilege to become Saints as a Son of God and develop an intimate relationship with Him **[Psalms 91:1-2].** The LORD predestined and elected to use this approach to redeem a fallen world. The decision to takes God offer is left to us. His desire is that all men received salvation **[1 Timothy 2:4].** If we were already predestined, He would not have the desire for all men to receive salvation.

Things to Think About. In the space below, write your spiritual thoughts and the revelation from this flawed truth:

_____

_____

_____

_____

_____

_____

_____

FLAWED TRUTH#5

Who is the Holy Spirit?

We seldom discuss the Holy Spirit because we have been accustomed to saying it in the name of Jesus. Now, we understand the meaning of "in the name of Christ." Jesus proclaims a contract that we act as His Power of Attorney on earth. So, we say by the power and authority given unto me by Christ Jesus. However, we can have kingdom authority and yet be spiritually weak and ignorant of God's ways.

Therefore, Abba Father's remedy at Jesus Christ's departure from earth was to give us the **"Holy"** Spirit. Why **"HOLY"** Spirit and not just Spirit?

- Holy- Hebrew = "*Kodesh*" Set apart and distinct.
- God is a Spirit **[St. John 4:24]. God is Holy [I Peter 1:16].**
- The Holy Spirit is God's Spirit in us to sanctify (set us apart) from the world so we can worship Him in Spirit and truth **[St. John 4:24].**

The Holy Spirit is given to us because of our fleshy nature **[Galatians 5:17].** Because of our LUST. **17 For what the flesh wants is opposed to the Spirit. What the Spirit wants opposes the flesh. They are opposed to each other, and so you do not do what you want to do.** Therefore, we need to know the Holy Spirit. The devil has released many spirits into the world **[I John 4:1-6].**

The Holy Spirit [St. John 14:16-20].

- o Christ Jesus on earth could only deposit one measure of grace at a time, but Yahauh (God) could deposit His Holy Spirit into the soul of any believer, so He could always be with us all **[St. John 14:16].**
- o Another Comforter {Advocate) [St. John 14:16]. He does what Jesus Christ would do if He were with us [I John 2:1].
- o Comforter– Hebrew = *Ha-Melitz* = to intercede

The Holy Spirit allows us to have constant contact with God instead of relying on someone (Jesus Christ) outside of us to strengthen us **[St. John 14:.17].** The Holy Spirit seizes us from darkness and strengthens us to have more of God. Have you had those encounters with God where you feel His presence surrounding and consuming you? When that moment has passed, we often long for that feeling of power and peace again.

The Holy Spirit allows constant contact with God to be a lifestyle **[St. John 14:17].** When you set your affections of things above, the Holy Spirit keeps us in relationship with Abba Father **[Colossians 3:2].** Do we receive the Holy Spirit when we confess Christ and are saved? NO. After we hear the word of truth, the gospel of our salvation, and after we believe, we are sealed with the Holy Spirit of promise **[Ephesians 1:13].** This seal removes the enmity God has for the world.

HOLY SPIRIT IS GIVEN IN ONE OF TWO DIMENSIONS. **FILLED AND FULL.**

- **Filled with the Holy Spirit**

    o You must ask God to fill you with His Holy Spirit **[St. Luke 11:13].**

    o The Apostle Peter was filled with the Holy Spirit on Pentecost but was still prejudiced [Acts 2:4, **10:28].**

    o When a believer is filled, he has all of the Holy Spirit, BUT the Holy Spirit may not have all of them.

- **Full of the Holy Spirit**

    o Prerequisite for a calling **[St. Luke 4:1]**
    o Prerequisite for leadership **[Acts 6:3].**

How does one become full of the Holy Spirit **Acts 11:23-24** gives us the "secret sauce" motivates God to not fill us but make us full of the Holy Spirit? Let us examines the qualification in this scripture.

- "Good" man – man that fit the purpose of God
- Full of faith
- Cleave to the Lord. Cleave mean just like skin.
- Manifest the fruit of the Spirit **[Galatians 5:22].**

Things to Think About. In the space below, write your spiritual thoughts and the revelation from this flawed truth:

_____

_____

_____

_____

_____

FLAWED TRUTH #6

Is it the Lord's Supper?

Many Christians partake in the Lord's Supper around the world and do not have a clear understanding of what it is, why we do it, and what it does for us. This is our attempt to understand the power behind the Lord's Supper.

The Bible does not reference a Communion Table, but it is the Lord's Table or Passover Table. Nor IS IT CALLED THE LORD'S SUPPER. It is called the Passover or Lord's Table [St. Luke 22:11, I Corinthians 10:21]. **There are three tables in the New Testament church as follows:**

1. The Benevolence table
2. The Lord's Table or Passover Table
3. The Pastor's table.

Communion is a practice or ritual that uses bread and wine as a symbol for Christ's blood and for His body. This is truth but it is flawed.

The word "Communion" in Hebrew is *davak* and means fellowship. That is why it is seen as ritual or a practice. WRONG name for most important covenant in the Bible.

This error is taking out of context when Apostle Paul talks about idolatry and mentions communion of the body and blood of Christ [I Corinthians 10:14 - 16]. The early church turned the Lord's Table into Communion. The early church was having supper and made it a feast. Paul accused them of making the Lord's Table into the Lord's Supper [I Corinthians 11:20-22]

Therefore, Communion and the Lord's Supper is FLAWED truth. What is the big deal, it is only a name right? [Deuteronomy 4:2].

Many churches changed the context, and many followed. The Lord's Table in **St. Matthew 26** is more than a ritual or just fellowship with Christ Jesus as an ordinance. It represents a new testament between God and us.

Christ gave us a new testament between God and us [St. Mathews 26:26-29].

- It is a New Testament – Testament –Hebrew = *berit* = contract or covenant.
- A new covenant in blood [St. Luke 22:20].
- The covenant or testament is God's will, a contract with God. God has granted us a NEW WILL to replace His OLD WILL or testament [Hebrews 9:18-22].

God made the first or OLD covenant at Passover [Exodus 12:1-7, 13]. It consisted of blood and bread.

- Christ makes the new covenant at Passover [St. Matthews 26:19-20]. It consisted of blood (wine) and bread. We no longer have to use blood because of Christ [Hebrews 9:25-28].

- **We are instructed to use wine.**

The Lord's Supper is the new covenant or contract with God through Christ Jesus.

- A covenant [God's will] is only legitimate through the death of the Testator **[Hebrews 9:13-18]**.

In the Old Testament Covenant – PASSOVER. God promised He would remember His promise of redemption when He saw the blood and unleavened bread at Passover **[Exodus 12:13]**.

- God commanded the Hebrews to keep this covenant forever **[Exodus 12:14]**
- No plaque be upon you
- Protect us from the plaques that God sent to destroy the unrighteous.

God did NOT change His plan; He changed His method **[Malachi 3:6]**.

In the New Testament Covenant – PASSOVER. Christ, the ultimate and final sacrifice, obtained eternal redemption with His body and blood **[Hebrews 9:11-13]**. We receive the exact promises of **Exodus 12:13-14** through one sacrifice.

Each time we participate in this new covenant, it reminds God of His contract with us, His will for our life, and the remission of our sins **[St. Matthews 26:28]**.

- Remission – Hebrew = *shemittah* = dismissal

Why is the Lord's Table important?

In our new covenant with God, Christ promised abundant life on earth and eternal life with the Father **[St. John 6:53-58]**.

The Lord's Table reaffirms the contract or covenant between God and us, like the Passover in Exodus **[I Corinthians 11:27-30]**.

1. We 'show the Lord's death" to who? To God, like in the book of Exodus 12 chapter.

2. **THE LORD'S TABLE IS NOT A RITUAL**. God warns us against taking communion without considering what it means and why we are doing it. The intent is not for us to mindlessly perform a ritual, [I Corinthians 11: 30]—weakness, sickness, death.

3. "Do this in remembrance of me" Remember what? We focused too long on what He did and not why He did it. Christ brought us to God through the death of his body and shedding of blood **[I Peter 3:18]**.

Things to Think About. In the space below, write your spiritual thoughts and the revelation from this flawed truth:

_____

_____

_____

_____

_____

_____

_____

_____

_____

_____

_____

_____

FLAWED TRUTH#7

Why Baptism?

We boldly declare that there are two ordinances in the Christian church: Baptism and the Lord's Table.

What is an ordinance? An ordinance is a sacred, formal act or ceremony performed by the authority of the priesthood.

Many teach us that baptism symbolizes a Christian's belief in the work of Jesus Christ. It is a picture of the forgiveness of sins, not the actual forgiveness of sins. It is a sign to everyone that you follow Christ. Whereas this is the truth, it is flawed.

If it is a symbol or a ceremony, why did Christ receive baptism, and He made it a commandment?

- Jesus Christ commanded baptism [**St. Matthews 28:19-20**].
- Jesus Christ was baptized [**St. Matthews 3:13-17**]. **Why? He had no sin.**
- **St. Matthews 3:15** says to fulfill all righteousness

  o Righteousness – means that God consistently does what is consistent with His Character.
  o **St. Matthews 6:33**. God's righteousness. Act consistent with God's character.
  o God's beloved Son – Hebrew =**Ahoov** = MOST loved by God.

There is a deeper revelation to understand why God requires baptism. Peter emphasized that baptism was part requirement for receiving the Holy Spirit [**Acts 2:38-39**].

What is the purpose of baptism?

God uses natural things to explain spiritual revelation—Blood and water. We have received the revelation of the blood. Now, let us examine the water.

- A natural baby is born in water [St. John 3:4]. The woman's water breaks.
- A spiritual baby is born in water and spirit [St. John 3:5-6].

Only in baptism can we be buried with Christ in His death, burial, and resurrection. While under the water, we join Him in His likeness. We are buried with Him; in that burial, we also die and are crucified. Then, we are raised with Him. We become God's beloved child, and He becomes pleased with us [**Colossians 2:10-14**].

- He quickens us with Christ
- He forgives us of all our trespasses
- Blots out all ordinances that were against us and nailed them to the Cross

Peter says baptism saved us by affecting our minds through a good conscience toward God [**I Peter 3:20- 21**].

Paul explained that God led Israel through the Red Sea for their baptism. Just like faith to walk through the Red Sea delivered Israel from the bondage of Pharaoh and Egypt, faith in water baptism frees us from the bondage of sin by the devil **[I Corinthians 10:1-4].**

- The Pillar of Cloud that followed them was Christ **[Exodus 13:1, Exodus 14:19].**
- Since there was no ordinance when Moses led Israel's children through the Red Sea for their baptism, the Holy Spirit shows us how baptism fits in between Israel and Christians. Everyone baptized into Moses was saved from Egypt **[Exodus 14:29-30]**
- God used water to save Noah, the Children of Israel, and God used water to save us **[I Peter 3:20-21]**

When we are baptized, we are no longer slaves to sin. For He who died He freed us from sin **[Romans 6:3-11]**

Through baptism, we are baptized into Christ **[Galatians 3:27-29].** Baptism is how we put on Christ. We become the beloved of God. This is God's righteousness.

After baptism into Christ, we were no longer enslaved people to sin **[Romans 6:5-6}.** Sin after that is sin by choice.

When we are baptized, we are baptized into Christ. Baptism of water and the Holy Spirit gives us the right to enter the Kingdom of God [God's rule and authority] **[St. John 3:5].**

Kingdom God is peace and joy in the Holy Ghost **[Romans 14:17].** The Kingdom of God moves us from God's blessings to God's Favor. We become God's beloved Son.

Things to Think About. In the space below, write your spiritual thoughts and the revelation from this flawed truth:

_____

_____

_____

_____

_____

_____

_____

FLAWED TRUTH #8

How to Repent

People, preachers, and family tell us to repent. Usually, we are adamant that people repent of their fleshly sins. However, we must REPENT of ALL sins. There are fleshly sins; we know when we commit them. Then, there are sins of the spirit. We must acknowledge the sins of the spirit and not cause God to hinder our blessings.

I John 1:9, 10 instructs that God is faithful to forgive us and cleans all of our sins if we confess them. The problem is that the sins of the spirit are not visible to us. These sins are ATTIUTUDE sins. **Unfortunately, the sins of the spirit are more dangerous.** This is because they are not outward, public, or visible to us. These are the sins that the devil nurtures in us to make us feel holy. The Bible warns us about sins of the flesh, but God hates sins of the spirit **[Proverbs 6:16-19].**

We focus on faith, salvation, grace, prosperity, favor, etc., but we must concentrate on REPENTANCE. We cannot fully receive God's divine favor, abundance on earth, and eternal life until we repent.

WHAT IS REPENTANCE?

Before we examine what repentance is, we must examine what repentance is not. Repentance is not about feeling bad or guilty or expressing that I will never do it again. It does not mean turning away from sin. Sin is always present **[Romans 7:21-23].**

What does the bible say about repenting or repentance? **[Acts 3:17- 20].** Until we repent, then,

- Our sins are not wiped away
- God will NOT refresh (restore, recover, recuse) us

[Acts 3:17- 20]. Repent, then, and turn to God, so that your sins may be wiped out, that times of refreshing may come from the Lord.

- **Repent – Hebrew =*teshuvah* = return
- *Teshuvah* means more than turn away from sins. It means RETURN TO GOD'S RIGHTEOUSNESS.
- **Righteousness – Hebrew -*seek* = justice – Just behavior

  o How do we render justice **[Micah 6:8]?**

HOW DO WE REPENT?

Focus on God's GOODNESS.

We focus on the sins but do not stop. However, we must focus on God's goodness [**Romans 2:3-4**]. Old church song said, "Think of His goodness to you.

- The goodness of God will make us REPENT (return to Him) [**St. Luke 15:17-24**]
- The goodness of God is available every day [**Romans 8:31-32**].
- We say thank you and express gratitude as a passing thought. We say God is good when everything is peachy, but we become silent when trouble, problems, or crises come.
- HOWEVER, we should <u>FOCUS</u> on His goodness [**Joshua 1:8**].

Focus on bearing FRUIT [ACTS 26:20].

- We focus on working in the ministry, which is necessary. However, when we leave the church, we must bear fruit.
- FRUIT – Hebrew =*Parah* – Good works
- If there is no fruit, there is no repentance [**St. Matthews 3:8**]
- Proved that we have changed by our good works [**Galatians 5:22-25**].

Take extreme measures [St. Matthews 5:29, 30].

- Get rid of or avoid some people, places, or things that cause attitudinal sins [**2 Corinthians 6:17-18**].

After learning the true meaning of repentance, George and Susan decided it was time to take a bold step of faith and turn their hearts entirely to God. They realized that repentance was more than just feeling sorry for their mistakes—it was a complete change of mind and direction, a heartfelt decision to turn away from sin and align their lives with God's will.

As they sat together, they confessed their struggles and shortcomings to one another, acknowledging areas where they had fallen short of God's standard. They prayed together with tears of humility and gratitude, asking God for forgiveness and the strength to obey His Word. Their decision to repent brought a sense of freedom and renewed hope as they felt the weight of guilt lifted and the assurance of God's grace and restoration settled in their hearts.

Things to Think About. In the space below, write your spiritual thoughts and the revelation from this flawed truth:

_____

_____

FLAWED TRUTH #9

Condemnation versus Judging.

What is the meaning of these scriptures, **St. John 5:22 and St. John 8:15-16?**

Neither of these scriptures deals with judgment. The focus is that we have no right to condemn anyone.

St. John 5:22

For the Father judgeth no man but hath committed all judgment unto the Son:

To understand this scripture

St. John 5:22, you must read **St. John 5:20-24. The context was not about righteous judgment but rather about condemnation.**

- CONDEMNATION- Hebrew – *Rasha* = Punish.
- JUDGE – Hebrew – *Shofet* – Rule over or control

The context was Christ telling a man to talk up his bed and walk on the Sabbath day **[St. John 5:10].** They condemned the man because of religion and Mosaic Law **[St. John 5:16].** The lesson is that we have no right or authority to charge anyone based on our view of righteousness. God is the only righteous JUDGE. We judge others on the things we do not do. Therefore, we believe we are better. We focus on the sins of the flesh and miss the sins of the spirit [[**Proverbs 6:16-19].** **God hates spiritual sins.**

Christ instructs the Pharisees and us that God does not condemn those who believe in Him **[St. John 5:24].**

St. John 8:15-16

[15] Ye judge after the flesh; I judge no man. [16] And yet if I judge, my judgment is proper: I am not alone, but the Father and I that sent me.

To understand this scripture, St. John 8:15-16, one must read **St. John 8:4-11.**

The context is about a woman caught in the act of adultery. The Pharisees used the Mosaic Law and said she should be stone. They condemned her.

Jesus said, "I judge no man." In the sense of merely condemning people, which is what the Pharisees were doing, Jesus judged nobody. The Savior did not need to come into the world to blame it; it was already condemned **[John 3:17].** Christ came to save the world and pay the penalty for sin through redemption by His dying in our place. Unless we are willing to do that, we cannot condemn.

LESSON: We cannot judge (control or rule over) or condemn (punish), but restore any Christian who falls in sin or sins **[Galatians 6:1-2].**

Things to Think About. In the space below, write your spiritual thoughts and the revelation from this flawed truth:

_____

_____

_____

_____

_____

_____

_____

_____

FLAWED TRUTH #10

Is Jesus in the Old Testament?

Many people ignore the Old Testament since they believe the name of Jesus does not show up. They suggest that Jesus Christ makes the New Testament relevant. Others claim that Jesus could not have been a natural person or God because they do not see His name written in the Old Testament scriptures.

To understand this question, we must UNDERSTAND the difference between **transliteration and translation. Our Bible is not a translation but a transliteration from Hebrew text.**

- Translation is attempting to produce meaning for meaning from one language to another
- Transliteration is reproducing a word or name from one language to another to produce the same sound or pronunciation

Jesus is the English transliteration of His Hebrew name. His Latin, Greek, or English name will NOT be found in the Old Testament.

The Old Testament is written in Hebrew and Aramaic.

- The Greek transliteration of His Hebrew name is **Iesous** [yay-SOOS].
- In the late 4th century, Jerome translated the Bible into Latin, a manuscript known as the Vulgate. In it, the Greek Iesous became the Latin *Iesus* [YAY-soos].
- In the 1611 Kings James Bible, the "I" was officially changed to "J" = Jesus [YEE-sus].
- In Hebrew, His name is Yahushua or Yeshua **(Aramaic).**

Therefore, the name **Jesus** is not a Greek transliteration but a Greek-to-Latin-to-English transliteration. The Modern English Bible is an English Transliteration of Old Testament scripture.

In the Hebrew **Tanakh**—the 24 books of the Old Testament, including the Torah—Christ is anglicized as Messiah [HaMashiach = Ha-Mah-SHEE-akh]. Anglicized means to make someone's name sound more like English by changing its spelling, pronunciation, or form. However, "Messiah" does not appear in the Torah (Books of Moses) or the **Tanakh**.

Some Biblical Scholars reference Jesus Christ as *Yeshua HaMhiach* (Yeh-SHOO-ah Ha-Mah-SHEE-akh), **anglicized** to mean "Jesus the Messiah."

What does Tanakh mean in Hebrew?

Tanakh is an acronym created from the first letters of the **T**orah, **N**evi'im, and **K**etuvim.

The Tanakh consists of three parts:

- Torah: The Hebrew word for law or instruction
- Nevi'im: 'prophets' in Hebrew

- Ketuvim: 'writings' in Hebrew

The Jews use the Tanakh as their sacred text. It has the same content as the Christian Old Testament, but the books are ordered differently.

Christ is NOT a name but a "Title".

- Greek = Christos =Anointed one or Chosen One.
- Hebrew – Mashiach = "King." **[Genesis 49:10, I Chronicles 17:11-14, Numbers 24:15-17].**

This is why the Jews rejected Jesus Christ because He said He was God; the Apostle and other Jews deserted Him or rejected Him because they were expecting a King to protect their nation from invaders and oppression.

The Bible challenges us to determine His name [Proverbs 30:4]. "What is his name, and what is his son's name, if thou canst tell?"

Jesus' Hebrew name is *Yehoshua,* abbreviated *Yeshua {Aramaic).*

- **Yehoshua, or Yeshua– Yehovah is salvation**
- **Hebrew – Mashiach = "King."**
- **Yehoshua Mashiach [Ha-Mah-SHEE-akh] = King of Salvation**

IN THE CHRISTIAN BIBLE.

When you see "the LORD" = Yahauh or Yehovah - The LORD is the God of the Bible. He is the Creator of all things and sovereign over all creation **[Psalms 148:13, Psalms 23:1]**

When you see "the Lord" – "Yeshua Mashiach" – King of Salvation **[St. John 13:13, Daniel 7:13-14, I Timothy 6:15].**

CHRIST IS IN THE OLD TESTAMENT REFERENCED AS "SALVATION."

To find Jesus Christ in the Old Testament, search the Hebrew text for Yeshua Mashiach or "King of Salvation."

Luke and the Apostle Paul state that *Yeshua* is in the Old Testament. The prophets give witness of Him **[Acts 10:43, Romans 3:21-22]. The Law and Prophets is the Old Testament.**

LET US EXAMINE A COUPLE OF EXAMPLES IN THE OLD TESTAMENT IN THE HEBREW.

Remember,

Yeshua = Salvation

Mashiach = King

A couple of Examples are as follows:

"Behold, The LORD hath proclaimed unto the end of the world, say ye to the daughter of Zion, Behold, thy salvation [Yeshua] cometh; behold, his reward is with him, and his work before him [Isaiah 62:11]."

I wait for Your salvation [Yeshua], O Lord [Genesis 49:10-11, 18].

The Scriptures describe God [Yah Oh] in many ways, and the Scriptures describe Yeshua Mashiach, King of Salvation, in many ways.

If you look in the Old Testament, you will find Him as Yeshua or Yeshua Mashiach, the King of Salvation, distinct from the figure of Jesus Christ. This distinction is crucial in understanding His identity.

Numerous references in the Old and New Testaments corroborate Yeshua and provide a wealth of evidence to support His identity.

Old Testament	Identified as	New Testament
Isaiah 7:14	Immanuel	St. Matthews 1:23
Numbers 20:10-13	Rock in the Wilderness	I Corinthians 10:1-4
Isaiah 43:3,10-11	Savior	*Titus 2:13*
Zachariah 9:9	King	*St. Mark 11:7-10*
Hosea 11:1	Place of Birth	St. Matthews 2:14-15

Things to Think About. In the space below, write your spiritual thoughts and the revelation from this flawed truth:

_____

_____

_____

_____

_____

CHAPTER 10

THE SECRET REVEALED

The pursuit of divine revelation has been a central theme in the spiritual journey of individuals across different faith traditions. Seeking a revelation from God involves a profound desire to connect with the divine, to receive guidance, insight, and a deeper understanding of one's purpose. This essay aims to provide a comprehensive guide on receiving revelations from God, drawing on theological, scriptural, historical, and practical insights to assist believers in their spiritual quest.

Before delving into the process of receiving revelations, it is crucial to grasp the nature of divine revelation. In theistic traditions, disclosure is a communication between the religious and human beings. This communication can take various forms, including direct personal experiences, inspired scriptures, visions, dreams, and the inner prompting of the Holy Spirit. Some individuals report direct encounters with the divine, experiencing God's presence tangibly. These encounters can be transformative, providing profound insights and a deep connection with the divine.

Scriptural Revelation:

The sacred scriptures are a primary source of divine revelation. These texts contain timeless truths and guidance directly inspired by the Divine. Spiritual revelations, often described as moments of profound insight and connection with the divine, have been a cornerstone of religious and philosophical traditions throughout history. These revelations serve as beacons guiding us toward a deeper understanding of their purpose, the nature of existence, and the divine presence.

Scriptural revelations are divine insights communicated through sacred texts. Documented in Holy Scripture, they serve as a guiding light for believers, offering profound insights into the nature of the divine, the purpose of existence, and the path to spiritual enlightenment.

Scriptural revelations are the sacred text comprising the Old and New Testaments. The Old Testament contains numerous instances of divine communication, including visions, dreams, and direct encounters with God. One notable example is Moses receiving the Ten Commandments on Mount Sinai **(Exodus 20).** The prophet Isaiah also experienced a powerful vision of God's glory in the temple **(Isaiah 6).**

The New Testament continues the theme of revelations, with the angelic announcement to Mary about the birth of Jesus **(Luke 1:26-38)** and the transfiguration of Jesus witnessed by Peter, James, and John **(Matthew 17:1-13).** The Book of Revelation, attributed to the apostle John, is a visionary account unveiling apocalyptic insights into the future and the ultimate triumph of good over evil.

Navigating the Waters of Biblical Interpretation with Care.

The Christian Bible, revered as the sacred text guiding the faith and practices of millions worldwide, contains a profound reservoir of divine wisdom and moral teachings within its pages. However, the dangers of misinterpreting its contents are ever-present, potentially leading to theological errors, misapplications of ethical principles, and even division within religious communities. This essay explores the risks associated with misinterpreting the Christian Bible and emphasizes the importance of accurate hermeneutics in preserving the integrity of its teachings.

Theological confusion and misguided beliefs.

Misunderstanding the Nature of God (Isaiah 55:8-9): The prophet Isaiah's declaration that God's thoughts are higher than human thoughts and His ways higher than human ways underscores the challenge of comprehending the divine. Misinterpreting passages that describe God's attributes may lead to anthropomorphism or an inadequate understanding of God's transcendent nature.

Misguided Christological Beliefs [Colossians 1:15-20]: Colossians presents an Christological hymn emphasizing the supremacy and divinity of Jesus Christ. Misinterpreting these verses could lead to misunderstandings about Jesus' identity, potentially veering into heretical beliefs that compromise the orthodox understanding of the Trinity.

Ethical confusion and moral missteps.

Selective Interpretation of Moral Imperatives [Matthew 22:37-40]: Jesus' command to love God and love one's neighbor as oneself encapsulates the essence of Christian ethics. Misinterpreting or selectively applying these moral imperatives may result in a skewed ethical framework, allowing for hypocrisy, discrimination, or neglect of crucial social responsibilities.

Justification for Discrimination (Galatians 3:28): The apostle Paul's assertion in Galatians that "there is neither Jew nor Greek, there is neither slave nor free, there is no male and female, for you are all one in Christ Jesus" underscores the Christian principle of equality. Misinterpreting such passages may lead to the justification of discriminatory practices, undermining the foundational idea of inclusivity within Christian teachings.

Division and Sectarianism:

Doctrinal Disputes and Denominational Division (1 Corinthians 1:10): Paul's plea for unity among the Corinthians highlights the potential for division within Christian communities. Misinterpreting doctrinal nuances or emphasizing minor theological differences may lead to schisms and the formation of denominations, fracturing the unity that should characterize the body of Christ.

Interpreting Apocalyptic Texts (Revelation 20:1-10): The Book of Revelation, filled with apocalyptic imagery, has been a source of much debate and speculation. Misinterpreting these texts may lead to misguided predictions about the end times, fostering fear, fanaticism, and the formation of sects centered on apocalyptic expectations.

The importance of contextual understanding.

Historical and Cultural Context (2 Timothy 2:15): Paul's exhortation to Timothy to rightly handle the word of truth emphasizes the importance of contextual understanding. Ignoring biblical texts' historical and cultural context may lead to misinterpretations, as the original meaning becomes distorted when divorced from its cultural backdrop.

Literal vs. Symbolic Interpretation (John 6:53-54): Jesus' metaphorical language about eating His flesh and drinking His blood in John 6 has led to various interpretations. Misinterpreting symbolic language as literal truth may result in doctrinal errors, such as misunderstandings about the nature of the Eucharist.

Guardrails against misinterpretation.

The Role of Tradition (2 Thessalonians 2:15): Paul's encouragement to hold fast to traditions reinforces the value of interpretive continuity within the Christian community. Understanding the interpretations passed down through the age safeguards against novel, potentially erroneous interpretations.

The Guidance of the Holy Spirit (John 16:13): Jesus' promise that the Holy Spirit will guide believers into all truth highlights the spiritual dimension of interpreting scripture. Prayerful reliance on the Holy Spirit's guidance safeguards against human biases and ensures a more accurate understanding of the biblical text.

Misinterpreting the Christian Bible poses substantial risks, ranging from theological confusion and ethical missteps to division within religious communities. The Bible's multifaceted nature requires careful attention to context, historical understanding, and the guidance of the Holy Spirit. By acknowledging the potential dangers of misinterpretation and adopting a humble and discerning approach to biblical hermeneutics, believers can strive to preserve the integrity of the sacred text and avoid the pitfalls that may arise when navigating the treacherous terrain of scriptural understanding.

Spiritual Revelations:

Spiritual revelations are transcendent experiences that provide individuals with profound insights into the spiritual or divine realm. These moments heightened awareness, a deep connection with the sacred, and a profound understanding of universal truths. Such revelations can manifest in various forms, including visions, dreams, mystical encounters, or an overwhelming sense of inner enlightenment.

The significance of spiritual revelations.

Personal Transformation: Spiritual revelations can catalyze transformative changes in an individual's life. Through these experiences, individuals often gain clarity about their purpose, overcome personal challenges, and undergo a process of inner purification.

Connection with the Divine: These revelations foster a deeper connection with the divine or spiritual realm. Through direct communion with the sacred, individuals may experience a sense of oneness and unity with the cosmic order, transcending the boundaries of the material world.

Guidance and Wisdom: Spiritual revelations often provide profound insights and advice, offering a source of wisdom that can help individuals navigate the complexities of life. Many religious and spiritual leaders attribute their teachings and ethical principles to the insights gained through spiritual revelations.

Faith and Hope: Experiencing a spiritual revelation can strengthen an individual's belief and instill a sense of hope. The assurance gained from these encounters can sustain individuals during times of hardship, providing a source of resilience and inner strength.

Visions and Dreams:

Throughout history, individuals have reported receiving revelations through visions and dreams. These experiences often involve symbolic imagery that carries profound spiritual meaning.

Visions and dreams, as mysterious and ethereal as they may seem, have held significant importance in various religious and spiritual traditions throughout history. These transcendent experiences often serve as a conduit for divine communication, offering insights into the spiritual realm and guiding individuals on their faith journeys.

The Bible contains numerous instances of visions and dreams as a means of divine revelation. The prophet Joel spoke of a time when God would pour out His Spirit, leading to visions and dreams among people (Joel 2:28). The New Testament recounts Joseph's dreams foretelling the birth of Jesus (Matthew 1:20-21) and the visions experienced by the apostle Peter, such as the vision of unclean animals (Acts 10:10-16), signaling a shift in understanding about God's inclusive plan.

Visions and dreams, integral elements of divine communication, play a significant role in the Christian Bible. Throughout the Old and New Testaments, individuals experience profound encounters with the sacred through these ethereal channels. This essay explores the rich tapestry of visions and dreams in the Christian Bible, examining their significance, patterns, and transformative impact on individuals and the course of biblical history.

Old Testament visions and dreams: portals to divine revelation.

Abraham's Vision of Covenant (Genesis 15:1-6): The patriarch Abraham, a central figure in biblical history, received a visionary encounter with God. In a deep sleep, God revealed to Abraham the covenant He intended to establish. The vision included a promise of descendants as numerous as the stars, symbolizing the future nation of Israel. Abraham's faith in God's vision counted as righteousness.

Jacob's ladder (Genesis 28:10-22): Jacob, the grandson of Abraham, experienced a remarkable dream at Bethel. In this vision, he saw a ladder reaching from earth to heaven, with angels ascending and descending. God affirmed the covenant with Jacob, promising him land and numerous descendants. Jacob, upon awakening, recognized the sacredness of the place and set up a pillar as a symbol of his encounter with the divine.

Joseph's Dreams (Genesis 37:5-11): Joseph, son of Jacob, was gifted with the ability to interpret dreams. His dreams, depicting his family bowing down to him, foreshadowed his future role in

Egypt. Despite causing resentment among his brothers, these dreams became instrumental in God's providential plan to preserve Jacob's family during a severe famine.

Moses and the Burning Bush (Exodus 3:1-15): Moses encountered God through a burning bush not consumed by the flames. God commissioned Moses to lead the Israelites out of Egypt in this vision. The revelation of God's sacred name, "I AM WHO I AM," marked a pivotal moment in biblical history, highlighting the divine presence and authority.

Prophetic Visions (Ezekiel 1:1-28): The prophet Ezekiel experienced elaborate visions of divine glory, including the famous vision of the wheels within wheels. These complex images conveyed profound truths about God's sovereignty, the exiled Israelites' destiny, and the restoration of the divine presence among them.

New Testament visions and dreams: The unfolding of redemption.

The Annunciation to Mary (Luke 1:26-38): The angel Gabriel appeared to Mary, announcing the miraculous conception of Jesus through the Holy Spirit. Mary's acceptance of this divine message marked the initiation of the incarnation, a pivotal event in Christian theology.

Joseph's Dream (Matthew 1:18-25): Joseph, betrothed to Mary, received a dream affirming the divine nature of Mary's pregnancy and instructing him to take her as his wife. This dream ensured the fulfillment of prophecies and safeguarded the earthly upbringing of Jesus.

The Transfiguration (Matthew 17:1-13): Peter, James, and John witnessed the transfiguration of Jesus on a mountain, where His appearance changed, and Moses and Elijah appeared alongside Him. This extraordinary vision affirmed Jesus' divine identity and the continuity between the Old Testament Law (represented by Moses) and the Prophets (represented by Elijah) with the ministry of Jesus.

Paul's Conversion on the Road to Damascus (Acts 9:1-19): Saul, a zealous persecutor of early Christians, experienced a blinding light and heard the voice of Jesus on the road to Damascus. This vision led to his conversion, and he became the apostle Paul, a key figure in the spread of Christianity.

Peter's Vision of the Clean and Unclean (Acts 10:9-48): The apostle Peter received a vision of a sheet descending from heaven containing animals considered unclean under Jewish dietary laws. God instructed Peter to eat, symbolizing the inclusion of Gentiles in the divine plan of salvation. This vision was crucial to the early Christian community's understanding of God's inclusive grace.

The Role of the Holy Spirit: The Holy Spirit is often associated with the revelation of divine truths through visions and dreams. The fulfillment of Joel's prophecy in **Acts 2**, where the God poured out His Spirit on all people, is marked by visionary experiences, emphasizing the Holy Spirit's transformative power in believers' lives.

In the Christian Bible, visions and dreams serve as conduits of divine communication, bridging the gap between the earthly and the spiritual realms. From the patriarchs of the Old Testament to the apostles of the New Testament, individuals experienced these ethereal encounters as a means of receiving guidance, commissioning, and insights into the divine plan.

Inner promptings of the Holy Spirit.

In Christian theology, the Holy Spirit is the divine guide leading believers into all truth. Inner prompting, nudges, or a firm conviction are manifestations of the Holy Spirit's guidance.

Receiving a revelation from God begins with cultivating a receptive heart and mind. This involves creating an environment that allows openness, humility, and a genuine desire to hear from the divine. Humility is a foundational attitude for receiving divine revelation. Acknowledging one's limitations and surrendering the ego opens the door to a more profound connection with the sacred. In **James 4:6 (NIV),** it is written, "But he gives us more grace. That is why Scripture says: 'God opposes the proud but shows favor to the humble.'"

Creating moments of stillness and silence is essential for tuning into the subtle whispers of the divine. **In Psalm 46:10 (NIV),** believers are encouraged to "be still and know that I am God." Practices such as meditation, contemplative prayer, and mindfulness can aid in quieting the mind and fostering receptivity.

The intention behind seeking a revelation matters. Approach the divine with sincerity, authenticity, and a genuine desire to align with God's will. In **Matthew 6:6 (NIV),** Jesus advises, "But when you pray, go into your room, close the door, and pray to your unseen Father. Then your Father, who sees what is done secretly, will reward you."

Spiritual practices serve as vehicles for deepening one's connection with the divine and creating a receptive space for revelations. These practices vary across religious traditions but often share common elements aimed at fostering spiritual growth. Prayer is a universal spiritual practice that involves communication with the divine. Whether through formalized prayers, spontaneous conversations, or contemplative prayer, engaging in a regular prayer practice provides an avenue for seeking and receiving guidance. In Philippians 4:6-7 (NIV), believers are encouraged to "not be anxious about anything, but in every situation, by prayer and petition, with thanksgiving, present your requests to God."

Meditation and contemplation involve focused attention and reflection, creating a space for inner silence. Practices like mindfulness meditation, Lectio Divina, or other contemplative techniques can help individuals attune their hearts and minds to receive insights from the divine.

Fasting is a practice in various religious traditions and involves abstaining from food or other indulgences for a set period. Fasting consists of intensified prayer and reflection. Fasting is mentioned in the Bible as a means of seeking God's guidance, as seen in **Joel 2:12 (NIV):** "Even now," declares the Lord, 'return to me with all your heart, with fasting and weeping and mourning.'"

Delving into sacred scriptures is a profound way to encounter divine revelation. Reading, studying, and meditating on scripture allows individuals to engage with the inspired words that carry timeless truths. **2 Timothy 3:16-17 (NIV)** affirmed, "All Scripture is God-breathed and is useful for teaching, rebuking, correcting and training in righteousness."

Rituals and sacraments hold significance in many religious traditions as tangible expressions of spiritual devotion. Whether it be the Eucharist, baptism, or other sacred rituals, these practices can serve as moments of connection with the divine.

In pursuing revelations, discernment is a crucial skill. Not every thought, emotion, or inner prompting necessarily originates from the divine. The Bible encourages believers to test their spirits to ensure that the guidance received aligns with God's truth. Comparing insights obtained with the teachings of sacred scriptures provides a reliable benchmark for discernment. In **1 John 4:1 (NIV),** believers are advised, "Dear friends, do not believe every spirit but test the spirits to see whether they are from God because many false prophets have gone out into the world."

Seeking guidance from wise and spiritually mature individuals can provide valuable perspectives and discernment. **Proverbs 11:14 (NIV)** states, "For lack of guidance a nation falls, but victory is won through many advisers." Divine revelations will align with God's character as revealed in sacred scriptures. If the guidance received promotes love, truth, and compassion and aligns with the foundational principles of faith, it is more likely to be in harmony with divine wisdom.

The journey of seeking revelations from God often requires patience and perseverance. Divine timing may not always align with human expectations, and persistent seeking is encouraged. Waiting on God with patient expectations is essential in times of apparent silence. **Isaiah 40:31 (NIV)** affirms, "But those who hope in the Lord will renew their strength. They will soar on wings like eagles; they will run and not grow weary; they will walk and not be faint." Jesus, in his teachings, emphasized the importance of persistence in prayer.

George, Richard, and Cathy sat together in the warm glow of the evening, the conversation naturally turning to the role of the Holy Spirit in their lives. George leaned forward, his voice filled with quiet conviction. "You know, I've been thinking a lot about the inner prompting of the Holy Spirit. I used to overlook or dismiss it, but now I see how vital it is. The Spirit's guidance is like a compass, pointing us back to God when we are unsure of the way forward. Have you ever noticed how He nudges you in ways that seem small at first but end up making a big difference?"

Richard nodded thoughtfully. "Absolutely, George. I have experienced that more times, than I can count. Sometimes it is a persistent thought I cannot shake, other times it is a sense of peace or discomfort that helps me discern whether I am on the right path. The Holy Spirit does not usually shout; He whispers. In addition, those whispers often challenge us to step out of our comfort zones or address things we would rather avoid. I think that's part of why many people struggle to recognize His prompting—it requires stillness and willingness to act on faith."

Cathy, sitting back in her chair, chimed in. "For me, the inner prompting of the Holy Spirit has often felt like an unexpected clarity in moments of confusion. There have been times when I am praying about a decision, and suddenly, the answer becomes clear in a way I cannot explain. However, I have also learned that these promptings always align with Scripture. The Spirit will not lead us to do anything contradicting God's Word. That's been a key lesson for me—testing every prompting against what the Bible teaches."

George nodded in agreement. "That's a crucial point, Cathy. I think many people misunderstand the role of the Holy Spirit because they do not see the connection between His guidance and the

Word of God. The Spirit is not just about giving us warm feelings or mystical experiences but transforming us into Christ's likeness. And that transformation often starts with those quiet, persistent nudges calling us to live differently—to forgive, serve, and step out in faith."

Richard added, "Let's not forget how the Holy Spirit works through community. Sometimes, the prompting comes through a word of encouragement or wisdom from someone else. I have had moments where someone's insight confirmed something I was already sensing but was not sure about. That is why staying connected to the body of Christ is so important. The Spirit moves not just in individuals but also in the collective."

Cathy leaned forward, her expression earnest. "But how do you know it's the Holy Spirit, not just your thoughts or emotions? That's something I've wrestled with."

George took a moment before responding. "That's a great question. For me, it is about consistency. When it is the Holy Spirit, the prompting often leads to something that glorifies God, not me. It might feel uncomfortable or counterintuitive but it is always rooted in love, truth, and humility. In addition, as you said earlier, Cathy, it is never in conflict with Scripture. I also pray for confirmation. Sometimes, waiting and seeking God's timing can bring clarity."

Richard nodded. "I'd add that the Holy Spirit's promptings often bear fruit. Over time, you see the evidence—peace, joy, growth in character, or even breakthroughs you could not have orchestrated yourself. It is a learning process, though. The more you respond to those promptings, the more attuned you become to His voice."

Cathy smiled with a spark of understanding lighting up her face. "That makes sense. It is not about perfection but about being willing to listen and obey, even when it is hard. The Holy Spirit isn't just guiding us for our sake but for the sake of God's greater plan."

The three of them sat in reflective silence for a moment, the weight of their conversation settling over them. George finally broke the stillness. "When we truly listen and respond to the Holy Spirit, we're not just walking in step with God's will—we're participating in His work. That's an incredible thought, isn't it?"

Cathy nodded. "It is. In addition, it reminds me how important it is to stay sensitive to His leadership. Who knows what He might prompt us to do next?"

Richard smiled. "Whatever it is, one thing's certain—if it's from Him, it will be worth it."

CHAPTER 11

THE POWER OF SILENCE

In a world characterized by constant noise and the ceaseless clamor of modern life, the power of silence stands as a profound and often overlooked force. The Bible, a sacred text revered by millions, attests to the transformative nature of silence in various contexts. One must delve into the biblical perspective on the power of silence, examining key scriptures and illuminating its significance in spiritual, personal, and communal dimensions. As we explore the scriptural narratives and teachings, we will uncover the depth of meaning woven into the fabric of silence. This understanding inspires hope as we realize its potential to bring about profound and transformative encounters with the divine.

George and Richard decided to have dinner while their wives decided to go shopping. Their wives were always aware of the "hot" sales around the city. George and Richard waved goodbye and told them to remember their budget. Both women laughed and said, "Increase our budget, and we won't have to watch it." Richard said, "I guess we created that behavior." George laughed, saying, "I think we got trained to accept that behavior."

George and Richard sit in the family room and begin to reminisce about their journey to date. They had not realized that their past exposure to the scriptures was more of a topology than a revelation. "How do you study and receive a revelation from God's word," Richard asked. Richard's career, family, and church responsibilities had him constantly on the run. He would carefully listen at church. He would find time to read at home but did not feel he completely related the scripture to his life. Richard thought it operated in reverse. He could understand the Word of God after some drama, problem, or crisis occurred. Now that they were on this new journey to understand the God of the Bible and not the God of the church, He understood and instructed us in Proverbs 3:5 that scriptures are God's preventive actions by directing our path. George responded, "These biblical stories and heroes in the Hall of Faith were not for our inspiration." George quoted **1 Corinthians 10:11**, stating they were for our example.

George leaned back in his chair to share with Richard a new understanding of why we do not hear from God by and through His Holy Spirit. George had realized that he did not understand the power of silence. He thought he had to have his favorite Gospel songs playing in the background as he studied God's word or television. "I learned the power of silence," George said. George had read Psalms 46:10 and received clarity about the power of silence. He did not understand that we take away God's glory because we immediately intellectualize what we read or hear. However, George shared with Richard that God wants us to be still and know that only He has the answer for our every situation. "Pull out your Bible, and let's examine it to understand that God wants us to be silent before Him.

Let us go to church, George, Richard said. There is a special meeting tonight. Perhaps we can go and learn about silence. It is not our meeting, so we can only talk and listen. "Great idea, Richard. We can sit in a quiet corner where no one will notice us," George said. All right, let us go and learn as they hurried to the car, "Richard responded.

The thoughtful silence to hear from God.

George and Richard sat in a quiet corner of the church, their Bibles open before them. The hum of activity in the church seemed distant, but the stillness of their conversation felt like an anchor amid life's chaos. George's words lingered in Richard's mind: *God wants us to be still and know that only He has the answer for our every situation.*

Richard, always eager to study Scripture, nodded and reached for his Bible. "So, you're saying that instead of rushing to find solutions, we need to pause and trust God for His guidance?"

George smiled. "Exactly. It is easy to fixate on our efforts and the hustle of fixing things. However, sometimes, God calls us to quiet our hearts and minds. He wants us to recognize that He alone holds the answers we seek."

George flipped open his Bible to Psalm 46:10, where the verse says, *"Be still, and know that I am God."* He paused, allowing the words to settle in their hearts. "This isn't just about being physically still. It's about stilling our thoughts, worries, and plans long enough to hear from God."

Richard leaned in. "So, it's not about waiting passively but being intentionally quiet to hear God's voice. How do we do that?"

"Good question," George said thoughtfully. "First, it requires humility. We need to admit that we do not have all the answers. We often feel pressured to do things independently, but God's invitation is to rest in His sovereignty. Look at Exodus 14:14—' The Lord will fight for you; you need only to be still.' It's a reminder that God is in control, even when things feel overwhelming."

Richard reflected on this. "It's hard sometimes, especially when facing challenges and wanting to take action. However, I see the wisdom in this. Being still means letting go of control."

"Exactly," George affirmed. "When we still our hearts, we make space for God to move. It is about trusting His timing and His ways. Isaiah 30:15 says, *'In repentance and rest is your salvation, and in quietness and trust is your strength.'* Our strength isn't in our ability to fix things but in our trust in God."

Richard looked down at his Bible, feeling the weight of those words. "So, being still isn't just a posture of waiting. It's an active trust in God's ability to intervene."

"Yes," George said, "and when we make room for God, we open ourselves to receive His wisdom and peace. Psalm 37:7 reminds us, *'Be still before the Lord and wait patiently for Him.'* It's not about rushing ahead or getting anxious, but about trusting that God has a perfect plan for every situation."

Richard's mind began to quiet as the truths from scripture sank in. He realized that he had often acted and found solutions quickly. Yet, the more profound truth was that God was already at work, even when Richard could not see it. In those moments of stillness, he could trust God's work more deeply than his own.

"Thanks, George," Richard said with a newfound peace. "This is a powerful reminder. Instead of trying to fix everything alone, I must still trust that God has everything in hand."

George nodded. "That's right. And when we do, we'll find that God's answers are often far greater than anything we could have come up with on our own."

As they sat quietly, the weight of God's presence surrounded them. The stillness was not just a physical pause but a moment of surrender—a surrender that allowed them to hear the whisper of God's guidance, peace, and wisdom as they read each scripture.

Psalm 46:10 - "Be still and know that I am God." This well-known verse from the Psalms encapsulates the essence of the contemplative silence that permeates worship. Being still before God implies deliberately quieting the mind and heart, creating a receptive space for the divine presence. This form of silence is not a mere absence of noise but an intentional hushing to acknowledge God's sovereignty.

Habakkuk 2:20 - "The Lord is in his holy temple; let all the earth be silent before him." The prophet Habakkuk emphasizes the sacredness of God's presence, calling for a collective silence before the Almighty. This communal hush signifies a shared recognition of divine majesty and invites believers into a sacred stillness where we hear God's voice.

Revelation 8:1 - "When he opened the seventh seal, there was silence in heaven for about half an hour." In the apocalyptic imagery of Revelation, the profound silence in heaven signifies a moment of awe and anticipation before the unveiling of significant events. This celestial silence underscores the gravity of divine actions and the transformative power inherent in stillness.

Richard stood in awe. He could not believe how far he had fallen short of the mark. He did not realize the power of silence. He imitated what he had seen as a boy and in church. After he prayed, he simply stood up and went about his planned or unplanned activities. God wants us to have silence and hear His voice speak to us through His Holy Spirit. The LORD wants us to hear Him. The LORD wants to participate in our lives.

God's intention from Genesis through Revelation is to dwell among us. His voice spoke to Adam in the Garden of Eden in the cool of the day **[Genesis 3:8-10]**. God instructed Moses to build a tabernacle in the wilderness so that He could dwell amongst the Children of Israel **[Exodus 25:8]**. God's most significant indication of His love for man was when He came in human flesh as Jesus Christ **[St. John 1:14]**.

Richard became upset. "Why hasn't anyone taught us this Spiritual principle, George?" Richard yelled. "Calm down, Richard. I am grateful for everything I learned in my spiritual growth. We are now endeavoring to become spiritually mature," George said. The revelations that Richard and George uncovered were foreign to everybody. However, too many people were giving God a cursory kind of worship. **Hosea 4:6** instructs us that God's people perish for a lack of knowledge.

George jumped into Richard's excitement. "We have to explore the power of silence fully. The Bible spends a lot of time talking about being silent in the presence of God," George said. Then, George pulled out his laptop and began typing the powerful thoughts coming to him.

In an era of constant connectivity and endless noise, silence can feel foreign, even uncomfortable. The hum of technology, social media chatter, and daily life demands surrounds us. Yet, amidst this cacophony, thoughtful silence opens the door to divine communion. For those seeking to hear from God, embracing silence is not just a luxury but also a necessity.

The concept of silence as a spiritual discipline is deeply rooted in Scripture. The Bible repeatedly highlights the importance of quieting our minds and hearts to commune with God. **Psalm 46:10** instructs us, "Be still, and know that I am God." This verse calls us to step away from the distractions of life and find peace in the stillness where God's presence exists.

The Prophet Elijah's encounter with God in **1 Kings 19** is another powerful illustration. After a dramatic display of wind, earthquake, and fire, Elijah finally hears God in a "still, small voice" or, as some translations put it, "a gentle whisper." God's voice was not in the noise but in the silence that followed. This narrative teaches us that God often speaks in ways that require us to be quiet and attentive to hear Him.

Practicing silence is increasingly difficult. We are bombarded with information from every direction—news, social media, advertisements, and even the internal noise of our thoughts and anxieties. This constant barrage can drown out the subtle voice of God, making it hard to discern His guidance and presence.

The challenge is not just the external noise but also the internal clamor. Our minds are often racing with worries, plans, and distractions. Even when we try to be silent, we find it hard to still our thoughts. Yet, this is where the practice of thoughtful silence comes into play. It is not merely the absence of sound but the intentional quieting of our spirit to be receptive to God's voice.

Thoughtful silence is a deliberate act of turning down the volume of the world and our minds to tune into the frequency of God's voice. It requires practice and discipline, but the rewards are profound.

Creating Space for Silence: Begin by setting aside regular time for silence. This could be early in the morning, late at night, or any time that allows you to be undisturbed. Find a quiet place to sit comfortably and focus on being present with God.

Quieting the Mind: Silence is not just about the absence of external noise; it also involves quieting the mind. This can be challenging, but techniques such as deep breathing, focusing on a single word or phrase (like "peace" or "Jesus"), or simply acknowledging and letting go of distracting thoughts can help. The goal is to create an inner stillness where God can speak.

Listening for God's Voice: In silence, listen not for an audible voice but for the subtle movements of the Holy Spirit within your heart. This might come as a sense of peace, a new insight, a conviction, or even a word or phrase that resonates deeply within you. God speaks differently, and thoughtful silence opens us to perceive His communication.

Journaling the Experience: After silence, consider journaling what you experienced. Write down any thoughts, feelings, or impressions that came to you. This helps solidify the experience and can serve as a record of how God speaks to you over time.

The benefits of thoughtful silence.

The practice of thoughtful silence has numerous spiritual benefits. It deepens our relationship with God, enhances our ability to hear His voice, and brings a sense of peace and clarity often missing in our noisy lives. Silence allows us to receive clarity on decisions, directions, and challenges. It can be hard to discern God's will when constantly bombarded with noise. Silence allows us to hear His guidance more clearly. Thoughtful silence fosters a deep sense of peace. When we take time to be still, we remind ourselves that God is in charge, and we can rest in His presence. This peace is a powerful antidote to the anxiety and stress that often accompanies our fast-paced lives.

Silence creates space for intimacy with God. In the quiet, we become more aware of His presence and more attuned to His love and grace. This deepened relationship with God becomes a source of strength and comfort in all areas of life. Regular periods of silence can lead to spiritual renewal. By stepping away from the noise and chaos, we allow our souls to refresh and revitalize. This renewal enables us to face life's challenges with a stronger faith and a more profound sense of God's presence.

While the benefits of thoughtful silence are clear, the practice itself can be challenging. Many people struggle with the discomfort of silence or the difficulty of quieting their minds. It is essential to approach silence with patience and persistence. Like any discipline, developing the ability to be still and listen to God's voice takes time.

One practical approach is to start small. Begin with just a few minutes of silence each day and gradually increase the time as you become more comfortable. Use Scripture, prayer, or a simple focus word to help center your thoughts. Remember that the goal is not to achieve perfect silence but to create space for God to speak.

Another challenge is the fear of what we might hear in the silence. Sometimes, God's voice may bring conviction, challenge, or call us to change. This can be unsettling, but it is also an opportunity for growth. Embrace the silence with an open heart, trusting that whatever God reveals is for your good and His glory.

Thoughtful silence is a sacred invitation to draw near God and hear His voice. This practice is a powerful way to cultivate a deeper relationship with the Creator in a noisy world. It requires intentionality and discipline, but the rewards are immeasurable. As we embrace thoughtful silence, we open ourselves to the gentle whisper of God. We find clarity in His guidance, peace in His presence, and renewal in His love. In the stillness, we discover that God has been speaking all along; we need to quiet our hearts to hear Him.

After George stopped typing, he sat back in his chair. Richard stared at him. "WE have missed the mark and fallen short of the glory of God," said Richard. "We have sinned. It is so paramount that we work to shut out all the voices but the Holy Spirit. We have been taught both directly and indirectly to play our gospel music. This approach is not what God ordained or demands. He demands that we stay on the listening side of prayer," George said. The listening side of prayer is shutting out all voices but the Holy Spirit.

Shut out all voices but the Holy Spirit.

As the conversation deepened, George turned to Richard, his expression earnest. "You know, Richard, when we talk about being still before God, we also have to realize that to hear Him truly, we must shut out every other voice. It's not just about physical silence—it's about silencing the noise inside and outside us."

Richard raised an eyebrow, intrigued. "What do you mean by that?"

George leaned back, his fingers tracing the edge of his Bible. "There's a lot of noise in this world—distractions, opinions, worries, and even our desires. In addition, often, these things drown out God's voice. To truly hear Him, we must consciously block out everything that isn't from the Holy Spirit."

Richard thought for a moment. "So, it's not just about being quiet, but about focusing solely on what God is saying to us through the Holy Spirit?"

"Exactly," George replied. "When Jesus said, *'My sheep hear my voice, and I know them, and they follow me'* (John 10:27), He wasn't just talking about hearing with our ears. He was talking about an intimate connection with the Holy Spirit. It's about tuning our hearts to His leading and becoming sensitive to His promptings."

He paused as if searching for the right words. "The Holy Spirit is our Helper, Guide, and Comforter. He speaks to us, but if we're overwhelmed by other voices—whether from the world, our own thoughts, or from fear and anxiety—we won't recognize His still, small voice."

Richard nodded, beginning to understand. "So, how do we shut out those other voices? How do we create space for the Holy Spirit to speak?"

George smiled, pleased with Richard's insight. "It starts with intentionality. First, we have to make the decision to stop filling our minds with the world's distractions. That means setting aside time for prayer and reflection, shutting off our phones, and intentionally seeking silence. However, it is more than that. We have to quiet our hearts from the inner noise—the doubts, the worries, the rush to have answers now."

Richard reflected on this. "It's like turning down the volume of everything else so we can hear God's quiet voice."

"Exactly," George said. "And this isn't always easy. The world constantly bombards us with information, advice, and pressure. However, turning our hearts toward God and His Word is the key. Scripture is how we can discern the Holy Spirit's voice. The Spirit never contradicts God's Word; instead, He confirms it and brings it to life in us."

George turned to 1 Kings 19:11-12, where Elijah encounters God. "Remember Elijah? He was looking for God in the wind, the earthquake, and the fire. However, where did he ultimately hear

God? In the still, small voice. That's how God speaks to us sometimes—not in the loud, dramatic moments, but in the whisper of the Holy Spirit."

Richard was quiet for a moment, contemplating this. "It makes sense. We can hear God more clearly in the stillness because we're not distracted by everything else."

George nodded. "Yes. And the more we practice being still and quiet before God, the more sensitive we become to His voice. It is about building that relationship with the Holy Spirit and recognizing His guidance. However, we cannot do that without constantly filling ourselves with everything else. We need to make space for God to move and speak."

Richard felt a sense of peace settles in his heart. He realized how often he had been too busy, too caught up in his thoughts and the noise around him. Now, he understood that to hear God clearly, he needed to actively shut out every other voice except the Holy Spirit's.

"Thanks, George," Richard said with renewed purpose. "I see now that hearing God isn't just about waiting quietly. It's about intentionally quieting everything else to focus on Him."

George smiled, placing a hand on Richard's shoulder. "Exactly. And when we do, we'll find that God's voice is clearer, more powerful, and more transformative than anything else we could hear." We are receiving these lessons from the Holy Spirit. Let's find some more scriptures," Richard said.

Job 2:13 - "Then they sat on the ground with him for seven days and seven nights. **No one said a word** to him because they saw how great his suffering was." In the face of profound suffering, Job's friends initially responded with a silence that spoke volumes. Their silent presence communicated a deep compassion and empathy that words could not convey. This compassionate silence illustrates the healing power of quiet companionship in times of anguish. These friends allow Job to hear from God before they begin to speak. Even though they did condemn him, they understood the power of silence.

St. Mark 5:36 - "Overhearing what they said, Jesus told him, 'Don't be afraid; just believe.'" In the story of Jairius' daughter, Jesus, upon encountering the mourning crowd, speaks words of comfort but also calls for a certain degree of silence—of trusting belief—in the face of adversity. This silent trust becomes a transformative force that contributes to the miraculous healing of the young girl.

Proverbs 17:28 - "*Even fools are thought wise if they keep silent, and discerning if they hold their tongues.*" The wisdom literature of Proverbs recognizes the power of silence in interpersonal dynamics. Remaining silent can sometimes convey more discernment and insight than a barrage of words. This form of silence is transformative in fostering understanding and resolving conflicts.

Richard was speechless. He had never heard that we should be silent before God. He was using habits and routines with God. He studied, prayed, and then rose to start another activity. He felt bad. Richard said, "I show grace to everyone but God. "I did not realize that God wanted to speak with me. He could only tell if I was listening. I could only hear if I were silent.

George immediately consoled Richard: "We are on this journey together, my friend." George realized no one had ever taught him how to pray or study the Bible. Initially, George felt guilty until he realized that, according to scripture, we perish for lack of knowledge. The power of silence allows us to hear from an omniscient, omnipotent, and omnipresent God—the only true and living God.

How can listening silently make us whole? This transformative power and the awe-inspiring beauty of silence fill us with hope and inspiration. God has met his people in silent moments **[1 Kings 19:12, I Samuel 3:3-4]**, encourages the practice of silence **[Psalms 62:1, Ecclesiastes 3:7]**, and even retreated to find silence himself [**St. Mark 1:35, St. Luke 5:16**].

George reassured Richard that, as Christians, we must retreat to sit silently in God's comforting presence. Sitting silently may not feel natural and uncomfortable, but God's presence can make it bearable, wrapping us in His comforting embrace.

Without silence, we struggle to know who God created us to be. When our minds fill with outside noise and inner thoughts, making space for the lessons that God, through His Holy Spirit, can teach us about ourselves and His work in the world each day becomes impossible.

When we commit to being quiet, silence becomes a tool for self-discovery. It helps us begin to notice all the things inside that we desire to come out—both positive and negative. People might dislike silence because they are not at peace with certain aspects of themselves. Silence can help us recognize what disrupts our peace, leading to introspection and contemplation.

Our world is busy and distracted. In this chaos, silence becomes a powerful tool that grounds us in our current reality and makes external matters less critical. It allows us to listen to God amidst the chaos of daily life, providing the spiritual grounding we need. By quieting the world and our minds, we try to let go of worries about the future and the past to sit with God as we are now.

Richard sat and looked at George in amazement. "My goodness, it all makes sense, George. We treat God like Amazon. We place an order and get busy with other things." "Yes, Richard. This is an important lesson we must learn on our journey to receive revelations for our soul," George said. George quoted a scripture that summed up the discussion. "Read **Isaiah 26:3**, Richard," George asked.

"Thou wilt keep *him* in perfect peace, *whose* mind *is* stayed *on thee*: because he trusteth in thee."

"When I read and understood that scripture, the puzzle pieces came together," George said. George realized that his mind was on his problems. He would pray to God to handle his situation. Now, he understood that he must keep his mind on the LORD and wait silently for direction. The Lord's direction brings peace to us. The challenge to overcome is learning to our understanding. Proverbs instructs us to acknowledge Him in all our ways, and He will direct our path.

George realized that the church conditioned us to praise Him but did not teach him the power of silence. It is challenging to achieve silence in such a noisy world. The world overwhelms us with noise. We can hardly find a place to reach this silence with God. Therefore, Jesus instructs us to go into our secret closet and close the door. The God who sees in secret will reward us openly.

Tears fell from George's eyes as he realized that he had brought the practices of the church home and not the practice of the Bible. God wants to spend personal time to develop a personal relationship. He wants to speak to our soul through silence. God desires a private but personal relation between Him and us.

Reflection.

Our world is busy and distracted. In this chaos, silence becomes a powerful tool that grounds us in our current reality and makes external matters less critical. It allows us to listen to God amidst the chaos of daily life, providing the spiritual grounding we need.

CHAPTER 12

WHAT YOU DO DEFINES YOU

In the complexities of life, the question of identity—"Who am I?"—is a perennial one. Philosophers, theologians, and everyday people have grappled with this question throughout history. At the heart of this inquiry lies the belief that our actions, the things we do daily, play a crucial role in shaping our identity. The Bible, a foundational text for millions, speaks profoundly to this truth, illustrating that what we do not only reflects who we are but also defines and molds us over time.

The Bible presents a holistic view of human identity, integrating being and doing. It affirms that humans are created in God's image **[Genesis 1:27]**, giving each person inherent dignity and worth. However, it also emphasizes that our actions are a critical expression of that identity. God calls us to live in ways that align with God's character and purposes, and our actions reflect our identity and are a means through which it is further developed.

In **Matthew 7:16-20**, Jesus teaches, "By their fruit, you will recognize them... every good tree bears good fruit, but a bad tree bears bad fruit... Thus, by their fruit, you will recognize them." Here, Jesus directly connects identity ("good tree" vs. "bad tree") with actions ("good fruit" vs. "bad fruit"). Our actions, the "fruit" we produce, reveal the true nature of our hearts and character.

Scripture consistently teaches that our actions are outward expressions of our inner selves. **Proverbs 23:7 says,** "For as he thinks in his heart, so is he." This proverb suggests that our thoughts, intentions, and desires shape who we are, and these internal realities inevitably manifest in our actions.

Jesus underscores this principle in **Luke 6:45**: "The good person out of the good treasure of his heart produces good, and the evil person out of his evil treasure produces evil, for out of the abundance of the heart his mouth speaks." This passage reinforces the idea that our actions directly result from what resides in our hearts. If we cultivate goodness, love, and faith within, our actions will reflect those qualities. Conversely, those traits will inevitably emerge in our behavior if we fill our hearts with selfishness, greed, or malice.

The Bible presents our actions as reflecting who we are and as a means of transformation. What we repeatedly do shapes who we become. In **James 2:26,** the apostle writes, "For as the body without the spirit is dead, so faith without works is dead also." James argues that actions evidence genuine faith; it is not enough to merely believe—our beliefs must be demonstrated through what we do.

This is not to say that our actions alone can save us—salvation, according to Christian doctrine, is by grace through faith **(Ephesians 2:8-9).** However, actions are the fruit of that salvation, the evidence of a transformed life. In **Romans 12:2,** Paul urges believers to "be transformed by the renewal of your mind," which leads to discernment and the ability to "test and approve what God's will is—his good, pleasing and perfect will." This transformation involves a change in thought and action, illustrating the deep connection between what we do and who we are becoming.

Obedience to God's commandments is a central theme in Scripture; Obedience shapes and refines us. In **John 14:15**, Jesus states, "If you love me, keep my commands." Obedience is presented not just as a duty but also as an expression of love for God. Consistently obeying God's word solidifies our identity as His followers. The story of Abraham in Genesis is a profound example of how obedience to God defines one's identity. Abraham's willingness to obey God's command to leave his homeland **(Genesis 12:1-4)** and later to sacrifice his son Isaac **(Genesis 22:1-18)** marks him as the "father of faith." Through these acts of obedience, Abraham's identity as a faithful servant of God is established and recognized. His actions defined him as a man of faith, a patriarch whose legacy is integral to the foundation of Judeo-Christian belief.

The Bible teaches that consistent righteous actions lead to the development of a godly character. In **Galatians 6:7-9**, Paul writes, "Do not be deceived: God cannot be mocked. A man reaps what he sows. Whoever sows to please their flesh, from the flesh, will reap destruction; whoever sows to please the Spirit, from the Spirit, will reap eternal life. Let us not become weary in doing well, for we will reap a harvest at the proper time if we do not give up."

This passage emphasizes the principle of sowing and reaping: our actions, over time, produce consequences that shape our character and, ultimately, our destiny. By consistently choosing to "sow to please the Spirit," we cultivate qualities like love, joy, peace, and self-control—traits that define a Christ-like character.

The apostle Peter also speaks to this process of character formation in **2 Peter 1:5-8,** where he urges believers to "make every effort to add to your faith goodness; and to goodness, knowledge; and to knowledge, self-control; and to self-control, perseverance; and to perseverance, godliness; and to godliness, mutual affection; and mutual affection, love." Peter's progression illustrates that each action and virtue builds upon the previous one, leading to a mature, well-rounded Christian identity.

Just as righteous actions shape and solidify a godly identity, sinful actions have the opposite effect, leading to identity corruption. **Romans 6:16** warns, "Don't you know that when you offer yourselves to someone as obedient slaves, you are slaves of the one you obey—whether you are slaves to sin, which leads to death, or to obedience, which leads to righteousness?"

Sinful actions, when practiced consistently, entangle a person and redefine their identity as one enslaved to sin. The life of King Saul vividly illustrates repeated disobedience and jealousy that led to his downfall. Despite being chosen by God and anointed as the first king of Israel, Saul's actions—his failure to fully obey God's commands and his attempts to kill David out of jealousy—ultimately defined him as a tragic figure whose identity was marred by disobedience and insecurity.

While our actions can lead to identity corruption, the Bible also offers the hope of restoration through repentance. In **1 John 1:9**, it is written, "If we confess our sins, he is faithful and just and will forgive us our sins and purify us from all unrighteousness." Repentance involves turning away from sinful actions and returning to righteous living. This behavior change accompanies a restoration of identity as a child of God.

The story of the Prodigal Son in **Luke 15:11-32** beautifully illustrates this process. The younger son's identity defined his reckless actions—demanding his inheritance, leaving home, and squandering his wealth in wild living. However, when he comes to his senses and returns to his father, he restores his initial identity. The father's embrace and the following celebration signify the restoration of the son's status as a beloved family member despite his previous actions.

This narrative highlights the transformative power of repentance. No matter how far one has strayed, returning to God in humility and repentance can redefine one's identity, restoring them to their rightful place in God's family. Jesus Christ provides the ultimate example of how actions define identity. Jesus' actions consistently reflected His identity as the Son of God and the world's Savior throughout His earthly ministry. From healing the sick to forgiving sins, feeding the hungry, and ultimately laying down His life on the cross, every action of Jesus was an expression of His divine identity and mission.

In **John 10:11,** Jesus declares, "I am the good shepherd. The good shepherd lays down his life for the sheep." His identity as the Good Shepherd defines His sacrificial action. Similarly, in **John 13:12-17**, after washing His disciples' feet, Jesus says, "Now that I, your Lord and Teacher, have washed your feet, you also should wash one another's feet... I have set an example that you should do as I have done for you."

Jesus' identity is inseparable from His actions. He taught about love, humility, and service and embodied these virtues through His actions. As followers of Christ, we are called to imitate His example, allowing our actions to reflect and shape our identity as His disciples.

The Bible teaches that what we do defines us. Our actions reflect our inner selves, are a means of character formation, and represent our identity. Motivated by love for God and obedience to His commands, righteous actions shape us into the people God created us to be. Conversely, sinful actions can corrupt our identity, but repentance and returning to righteous living offer the hope of restoration.

As believers, God calls us to live in a way that reflects our identity in Christ. This means consistently choosing actions that align with God's will, embodying the virtues of love, humility, and service, and being open to the transformative power of the Holy Spirit. By doing so, we honor God and allow our actions to define us as His faithful children equipped to fulfill His purposes in the world.

Ultimately, what we do is not just a reflection of who we are—it is a critical factor in who we become. Our actions, guided by the Word of God and empowered by His Spirit, are instrumental in shaping our identity and destiny. May we, therefore, be diligent in our actions, knowing that through them, we are continuously being formed into the image of Christ.

George understood the importance of identity through a journey of self-discovery and reflection. Growing up, he often found himself adapting to the expectations of others, masking his true self to fit into social circles or meet external standards. However, this left him feeling fragmented and uncertain about who he was. It was not until he experienced life challenges that George realized the value of embracing his unique identity. These moments of hardship forced him to confront his fears and question the core of his beliefs, passions, and values. He began to see that understanding and accepting his true self was essential for building authentic relationships and living a fulfilling life.

As George deepened his understanding of identity, he recognized its role in shaping purpose and resilience. By embracing his personal story, including strengths and vulnerabilities, he discovered a sense of clarity and direction. He learned that identity is an anchor in life's storms, providing a foundation for decision-making and a source of inner strength. This understanding transformed George's self-perception and allowed him to engage more meaningfully with others.

George walked through the front door, a sense of calm and clarity enveloping him after his conversation with Richard. Susan, sitting at the kitchen table with a cup of tea, looked up and smiled. "How was your time with Richard today?"

George sat down beside her, a thoughtful look on his face. "It was really eye-opening. We talked about something that's been on my mind a lot lately—identity. I realized something profound: our identity is like an anchor in life's storms."

Susan raised an eyebrow, intrigued. "An anchor? What do you mean?"

"Well," George began, "when we face challenges, difficulties, or even confusion, it's easy to feel lost or tossed around by the circumstances. But I came to understand that our identity in Christ is the anchor that holds us steady. It's the foundation we stand on when everything around us seems uncertain."

Susan nodded slowly. "So, our identity in Christ keeps us grounded, no matter what happens?"

"Exactly," George said, his voice growing more animated as he continued. "Think about it. If we don't know who we are—if we're constantly swayed by what others think of us, or by the ups and downs of life—we're like a ship without an anchor. However, when we know who we are in Christ, when our identity is rooted in Him, we have a foundation that cannot be shaken. It gives us clarity in decision-making, because we know what aligns with our true selves and what doesn't."

Susan took a sip of her tea, processing his words. "That sounds really powerful. But how do we make sure we're rooted in our true identity?"

George thought for a moment. "It starts with knowing what God says about us, not what the world or our circumstances try to define us by. In Christ, we are loved, forgiven, chosen, and free. Those truths do not change, no matter what happens around us. And when we understand this, we can make decisions from a place of confidence, because our choices reflect who we are in Him."

Susan leaned forward, her eyes thoughtful. "I can see how this would give you strength, especially in tough times. But what happens when we forget who we are or lose sight of that anchor?"

George sighed, his eyes reflecting a deep understanding. "It's easy to forget. Life gets loud, and we are caught up in all the distractions. However, that's when the storms feel the most overwhelming. Without our identity anchored in Christ, we are more likely to make decisions based on fear, comparison, or insecurity. However, when we remember who we are, it shifts our perspective. We don't have to be afraid of the storm anymore, because we know we're safe with God."

Susan sat back, reflecting on what George had said. "So, identity is more than just a label. It is the core of who we are. It shapes everything we do."

"Exactly," George said, his voice softening. "It's like a lens through which we see the world. When we know we are God's beloved children, it changes how we respond to others, how we handle stress, how we make choices. We are no longer driven by what we think we should be or by the world's expectations. We act from a place of inner peace and strength."

Susan smiled, a gentle warmth spreading through her. "I think I'm starting to get it. If we anchor ourselves in our true identity—who God says we are—then no storm can knock us off course."

"That's right," George said, reaching for her hand. "Our identity in Christ gives us stability, clarity, and strength. It's the one thing we can always count on, no matter what life throws our way."

They sat in silence for a moment; both reflecting on the depth of what George had shared. The noise of the world, the distractions, and the pressures of life could come and go, but the anchor of their identity in Christ would always hold them steady, providing the foundation they needed to face whatever storms lay ahead.

CHAPTER 13

THE SECRET PLACE

Psalm 91 is one of the most cherished chapters in the Bible, offering profound comfort and assurance of God's protection. Central to this Psalm is "the secret place of the Most High." This essay will explore the meaning of the secret place in Psalm 91, delving into its theological, spiritual, and practical implications. We will examine the context of the Psalm, the symbolic nature of the secret place, and how it applies to the lives of believers today.

Psalm 91 is a psalm of trust, often categorized as a psalm of protection. Theologians believe Moses wrote Psalms 91, although some traditions attribute it to David. The Psalm reflects a deep trust in God's power and promises, emphasizing the security and peace of dwelling in God's presence. The structure of the Psalm is poetic, with verses that build upon one another to create a vivid picture of God's protection. The imagery used—shadows, shields, and fortresses—conveys a sense of refuge and safety only found in God. The Psalmist's confidence in God's protection is unwavering, making it a powerful declaration of faith.

The phrase "secret place of the Most High" (Psalm 91:1) is a central theme in this chapter. It symbolizes an intimate relationship with God, where God hides and protects us under His divine care. The Hebrew word for "secret place" is *seter*, meaning a covering or a hiding place. This suggests a place of concealment, safety, and intimacy.

A Place of Intimacy: The secret place represents a close, personal relationship with God. It is where one can commune with Him away from the distractions and dangers of the world. This intimacy is not just about physical proximity but a deep spiritual connection. It is a place where the believer experiences the fullness of God's love, peace, and guidance.

A Place of Protection: The secret place is also a metaphor for God's protection. Just as a child feels safe and secure in a parent's embrace, God protects believers under the shadow of the Almighty. God protects His people from harm, danger, and evil in the secret place.

A Place of Rest: The secret place is a place of rest and peace. It is where the believer can find solace and refuge from the anxieties and challenges of life. In the secret place, a divine calm surpasses all understanding, a peace found only in God's presence.

God's Omnipresence: The secret place underscores God's omnipresence. It reminds us that God is always present with His people, offering protection and guidance. No matter where one is physically, one can dwell in the secret place of the Most High because God's presence is not a specific location.

God's Sovereignty: The secret place also points to God's sovereignty. God exercises His authority and power in the secret place, ensuring the safety and well-being of those who trust Him. The believer's security is not in their strength or abilities but in God's sovereignty.

Covenant Relationship: The secret place reflects the covenant relationship between God and His people. God reserves it for those who have entered into a covenant with Him, trust in His promises, and live in obedience to His word. Love, faithfulness, and commitment mark this relationship.

Dwelling in the Secret Place: The secret place concept is not just a theological idea but also a practical reality for believers. Dwelling in the secret place involves living in close communion with God, seeking His presence daily, and trusting in His protection.

Daily Communion with God: To dwell in a secret place, believers must cultivate a daily habit of spending time with God. This can be through prayer, meditation, reading the Scriptures, and worship. The secret place is not just a physical location but also a state of the heart and mind where one is constantly aware of God's presence.

Trust and Faith: Dwelling in a secret place also requires trust and faith in God's promises. It means relying on God for protection, guidance, and provision, even when circumstances are complex or uncertain. Trusting in God allows believers to rest assured that they are under His divine care.

Obedience to God's Word: The secret place is a place of obedience. To dwell in the secret place, one must live according to God's word, following His commandments and living a life that is pleasing to Him. Obedience is a crucial aspect of maintaining an intimate relationship with God.

Rest and Peace: Finally, dwelling in the secret place means experiencing God's rest and peace. In a world filled with chaos and uncertainty, the secret place offers a refuge where believers can find calm and tranquility. This rest is physical and spiritual, with a deep sense of peace from knowing that one is in the care of the Almighty.

The Secret Place and Spiritual Warfare: Psalm 91 also has implications for spiritual warfare. The secret place is where believers can find protection against spiritual attacks and demonic forces. The Psalm speaks of being delivered from the "snare of the fowler" and the "deadly pestilence" **[Psalm 91:3],** which can be understood as metaphors for spiritual traps and dangers.

Protection from the Enemy: The secret place is a fortress where God shields believers from the enemy's attacks. Just as a soldier finds refuge in a stronghold, believers find protection in the secret place of the Most High. This protection is physical and spiritual, guarding the believer's heart and mind from fear, doubt, and temptation.

Authority in Spiritual Warfare: Dwelling in a secret place also gives believers authority in spiritual warfare. The Psalm speaks of treading on the lion and the cobra (Psalm 91:13), symbolizing victory over evil forces. In the secret place, believers are empowered by God's presence to overcome their challenges and battles.

Divine Assistance: Believers receive divine assistance in times of spiritual warfare in the secret place. The Psalm mentions angels commanded to guard the believer in all their ways **[Psalm 91:11].** In the secret place, believers are not alone; heavenly beings support and help them in their spiritual journey.

The secret place in the New Testament

The concept of the secret place echoes in the New Testament, where the idea of dwelling in God's presence exists.

Abiding in Christ: In John 15, Jesus speaks of abiding in Him as the vine and the branches. This idea of abiding is similar to dwelling in a secret place. Just as the branch connects to the vine, believers connect to Christ, drawing life and sustenance from Him. This abiding relationship is essential for spiritual growth and fruitfulness.

The Indwelling of the Holy Spirit: The New Testament also speaks of the Holy Spirit dwelling in believers. This indwelling presence is where the believer constantly communes with God. The Holy Spirit guides, comforts, and empowers believers, enabling them to live a life that is pleasing to God.

The Kingdom of God: Jesus often spoke of the Kingdom of God as being within believers **[Luke 17:21]**. This internal reality is akin to the secret place where God reigns and where He establishes in the believer's heart and mind. The secret place is a physical location and a spiritual reality where God's Kingdom is present and active.

The secret place in **Psalm 91** is a profound concept that encapsulates the essence of a believer's relationship with God. It is a place of intimacy, protection, rest, and spiritual warfare. Dwelling in the secret place involves a deep, personal connection with God, marked by trust, obedience, and faith.

The secret place is not just a theological idea but also a practical reality that can be experienced daily. It is where believers can find refuge from the challenges and dangers of life, where they can rest in the assurance of God's love and care. In the secret place, believers are empowered to overcome spiritual battles, live in peace, and grow in their relationship with God.

Ultimately, the secret place points to the biblical theme of God's desire for a close, personal relationship with His people. It is an invitation to come into God's presence, to dwell under His shadow, and to experience the fullness of His love and protection. In a world filled with uncertainty and fear, the secret place offers a sanctuary of peace, security, and hope.

George and Richard understood the value of God's secret place through seasons of deep personal and spiritual trials. For George, the secret place became a sanctuary of peace during a tumultuous period. Struggling with overwhelming stress and uncertainty, he turned to prayer and meditation, seeking God's presence in the stillness of his heart. In those quiet moments, he experienced a profound sense of comfort and guidance that he could not find elsewhere. He realized that the secret place was more than a physical location—it was a sacred space where he could commune with God, find clarity, and be renewed.

For Richard, the revelation of the secret place came during a time of spiritual dryness and routine worship. Feeling disconnected from God, he yearned for a deeper relationship and began to carve out time to meet with God in solitude intentionally. As he poured out his heart in prayer and immersed himself in Scripture, he encountered God's intimate and transformative presence in a way he had never known before. Both George and Richard understood that the secret place was a refuge and a source of strength, wisdom, and direction. It became the foundation of their faith.

The phone rang, pulling Richard out of his thoughts. He glanced at the caller ID and saw Latasha's name flashing on the screen. He quickly answered, trying to mask his concern. "Hey, Latasha, how's everything going?"

"Dad, I don't know what to do," Latasha's voice was strained, filled with worry. "I've got this huge problem at work, and I don't know how to fix it. Nothing seems to be going right, and I'm getting overwhelmed."

Richard sat up straight, his heart going out to his daughter. Over the years, he had watched her face challenges, but this time, he sensed the weight in her words. "What's going on? Talk to me."

Latasha sighed heavily. "There's a big project that's completely falling apart. We are behind schedule, and the team is at odds with each other. The pressure is mounting, and I feel like I am failing. I do not know how to turn this around. I've tried everything I can think of."

Richard paused for a moment, letting her words sink in. He remembered his own struggles, how easy it was to get lost in the noise of the world and the pressure of trying to fix everything on his own. However, something he and George had talked about recently echoed in his mind—the secret place, the refuge where God's wisdom and direction flowed freely.

"Latasha," Richard said his voice calm yet firm, "I know you're facing something tough right now, but I want you to hear me. The solution is not going to come from your own strength or effort alone. You need to go into the secret place with God."

"The secret place?" Latasha asked a hint of confusion in her voice.

Richard smiled softly, his heart full of love for his daughter. "Yes, the secret place. It is that quiet, intimate space where you meet with God. It is where you lay down your worries, your frustrations, and your plans—and let Him speak to you. It is the place where His wisdom, peace, and direction flow. You have probably heard me talk about it before. But it's real, Latasha, and it's a place of refuge."

Latasha was silent for a moment, the weight of her father's words settling over her. "I don't know, Dad. I've been trying so hard to figure it all out on my own."

Richard understood. "I get that. However, the truth is, when we lean on our own understanding and strength, we often miss what God wants to show us. In the secret place, you do not have to have all the answers. You just need to show up, surrender, and let God lead. Trust me, He will show you the solution you need. Maybe it is a fresh perspective, maybe it is a change in how you are approaching the situation, or maybe it is peace in the midst of the chaos. But God's wisdom is always greater than our own."

"But what if I don't know how to do that?" Latasha asked, her voice tinged with doubt. "What if I don't know what to say?"

Richard chuckled softly, reassuring her. "It's not about the right words or a perfect prayer. Just be honest with God. Pour out your heart, tell Him what is going on, and ask Him for help. Sometimes, the quiet is enough for God to speak to you. Just be still, and listen. He'll lead you."

Latasha took a deep breath, the tension in her voice easing. "I think I get it now. I do not have to have all the answers myself. I just need to trust God with it."

"Exactly," Richard said, feeling a sense of peace settle over him as he spoke. "And remember, the secret place is always there for you. It is a refuge, a place of strength and clarity. Whenever you face a problem, big or small, go there first. God will show you the way."

Latasha was quiet for a moment before she spoke again, her voice softer now. "Thanks, Dad. I will do that. I really needed to hear that today."

"I'm always here for you," Richard said, his voice filled with love and confidence. "Now go into that secret place and let God show you what to do."

As the conversation ended, Richard felt a deep sense of peace. He knew that by guiding Latasha back to the secret place, he was helping her find not just the solution to her problem, but a deeper connection with the God who would lead her every step of the way.

George had been sitting quietly in the corner of the room, catching up on some notes, when Richard's phone call with Latasha caught his attention. Richard's voice was calm yet filled with a quiet authority, as he spoke to his daughter with wisdom and care. George could hear Latasha's frustration in her words, but as Richard spoke, something in his tone seemed to bring peace to the moment. There was a depth to what Richard was saying—something about a place of refuge, about God's direction coming from a secret place.

The more George listened, the more he found himself intrigued. He had always believed in the power of prayer and God's guidance, but Richard's words seemed to unlock something deeper, something more personal. George leaned in, absorbing every word.

"Go into the secret place with God and He'll show you the solution," Richard had said.

It was then that a revelation struck George like a wave crashing over the shore. He realized that the "secret place" was not just a metaphor or a nice idea—it was a tangible, sacred space where God's presence was real and accessible. George had always known the importance of seeking God in prayer, but now he understood that this secret place was not only about asking for guidance; it was about truly resting in God's presence, being still before Him, and trusting Him to provide what was needed, not just for the immediate problem but for every situation in life.

It was not that George had never heard of the "secret place" before, but today, hearing Richard speak so clearly and confidently, it clicked in a new way. George realized that it was in this space—

this intimate connection with God—that one could find not only wisdom and direction but also peace. The peace that passes understanding, the kind that calms the storms within and around us.

George reflected on how often he had rushed through prayer, eager to hear God's answers, but never really taking the time to *be* with Him, to let God speak without rushing in with his own thoughts and concerns. In the past, he had been so focused on the outcomes of his prayers—on finding solutions—that he missed the depth of communion God wanted to offer. The secret place was not just about seeking answers; it was about cultivating a relationship with God where His voice could be heard clearly, where His presence could be felt deeply.

Richard's conversation with Latasha had illuminated something George had not fully grasped before. It was not just the "solutions" that came from the secret place; it was the process of being still, trusting, and listening. In that space, the noise of the world faded away, and the clarity of God's guidance came into focus. George began to see that by taking time to be with God, he could not only solve problems but also deepen his relationship with Him, finding strength and wisdom for all areas of life.

He also realized that the secret place was not a one-time visit but a continuous invitation. It was not about finding a quick fix to a particular issue—it was about creating a habit of rest and trust in God's presence. Whether in the midst of a storm or in times of peace, the secret place was always available. God did not just meet George in moments of crisis; He wanted to meet with him daily, to offer direction and comfort in every moment.

Sitting there, George felt a renewed sense of purpose. It was time to embrace the secret place in a new way. He needed to intentionally carve out time to be still, to listen, and to rest in God's presence, not just for the answers, but also for the relationship itself. In doing so, George knew that God would continue to shape his heart, renew his mind, and provide the strength and direction needed for whatever life might bring.

Richard's words to Latasha had not only affected her but had become a revelation that was changing George's own approach to life and faith. The secret place was a refuge, a place where both strength and wisdom were found, and it would be the foundation of his faith moving forward.

CHAPTER 14

GOD CAN RESTORE LOST TIME

The idea of God restoring lost time is a theme deeply rooted in Christian theology, reflecting the belief that God can redeem and restore everything, including the time that seems wasted, lost, or stolen. Many people feel they have lost valuable time, whether due to poor decisions, sin, circumstances beyond control, or the passage of time. However, the Bible presents a God who is not limited by time and can redeem the years that the locusts have eaten [**Joel 2:25**]. This essay will explore the concept of God restoring lost time, examining biblical examples, theological implications, and practical applications for believers today.

Before delving into how God can restore lost time, it is essential to understand the biblical concept of time. The Bible presents time in several ways, reflecting its linear progression and cyclical nature. The Bible often presents time as a linear progression from creation to the end of the age. This is evident in the genealogies, historical narratives, and prophetic timelines that mark significant events in salvation history. Linear time moves from past to present to future, and within this framework, humans experience the progression of life from birth to death. In addition to linear time, the Bible reflects a cyclical understanding of time, particularly in the context of seasons, festivals, and the rhythms of life. **Ecclesiastes 3:1-8** famously reflects this cyclical nature, stating, "To everything, there is a season, a time for every purpose under heaven." This cyclical time emphasizes the repetition of specific patterns and the recurring opportunities for renewal and restoration. The Bible also introduces the concept of eternal time, which transcends the linear and cyclical. God exists outside of time, as in passages like **Psalm 90:4**, "For a thousand years in your sight are like a day that has just gone by." God's perspective on time differs from the human perspective, and His ability to interact with time is limitless.

Understanding these different aspects of time helps lay the foundation for understanding how God can restore what seems lost within the constraints of human experience.

The Bible contains numerous stories where God intervenes in the lives of individuals and nations to restore what was lost, including time. These stories are powerful reminders of God's ability to redeem and restore.

The Story of Job: One of the most profound examples of restoration is the story of Job. Job was a righteous man who suffered immense loss—his children, health, wealth, and reputation. However, after intense suffering and questioning, God restored Job's fortunes, giving him twice as much as he had before [**Job 42:10**]. While the lost years of suffering were undoable, God restored Job's future, blessing him with a long life and prosperity.

The Years That the Locusts Have Eaten: In **Joel 2:25,** God promises to restore the years that the locusts have eaten, a metaphor for the devastation that Israel experienced due to their disobedience. This promise is not just about physical restoration but also spiritual renewal. The lost years represented a time of judgment and loss, but God's promise of restoration brings hope that even redeems wasted years.

Hezekiah's Life Extended: The prophet Isaiah told King Hezekiah that he would die, but after praying earnestly to God, his life was extended by fifteen years **[Isaiah 38:5].** This is an example of God directly intervening to alter the course of time for an individual, granting them more time to fulfill their purpose.

The Prodigal Son: In the parable of the Prodigal Son **[Luke 15:11-32],** the younger son wastes his inheritance on reckless living, losing time and resources. Yet, when he returns to his father, his father fully restores him to his position as a son despite the time he lost in rebellion. The father's joy and the son's restoration illustrate how God's grace can redeem lost time. The idea that God can restore lost time carries significant theological implications. It speaks to God's nature, His sovereignty, and His grace.

God's Sovereignty over Time: God's ability to restore lost time underscores His sovereignty over all creation, including time itself. Unlike humans, God exists outside of time and can interact with it in ways that transcend human understanding. He can accelerate, decelerate, or redeem time according to His will. This sovereignty is a source of comfort for believers, as it means that no situation is beyond God's ability to redeem.

God's Grace and Mercy: Restoring lost time is a profound expression of God's grace and mercy. It is often in situations where we waste time due to sin or poor decisions that God's restorative power is most evident. God's grace not only forgives but also restores, giving back what was lost or stolen. This grace is unearned and reflects God's deep love for His people.

Hope and Redemption: Theologically, the restoration of lost time is a message of hope and redemption. It assures believers that God can redeem it no matter how much time has been lost. This redemption may not always look like a literal return of lost years but can manifest in renewed opportunities, relationships, and spiritual growth.

How God restores lost time today.

Understanding that God can restore lost time has practical implications for believers' lives. It affects how they view their past, present, and future and encourages them to live with faith and hope.

Redeeming the Time: Ephesians 5:16 urges believers to "redeem the time because the days are evil." This suggests that believers should live intentionally while, maximizing every opportunity to serve God and others. Even if time has been lost in the past, believers can redeem the present and future by aligning their lives with God's purposes.

Forgiveness and Healing: For many, the sense of lost time is tied to past mistakes, sins, or painful experiences. Understanding that God can restore lost time brings healing and freedom from regret. Believers are encouraged to seek God's forgiveness and trust in His ability to restore what was lost. This might involve healing relationships, restoring opportunities, or renewing joy and purpose.

Trusting God's Timing: Restoring lost time requires trust in God's timing. While humans often feel pressured by deadlines and the passing of time, God's timing is perfect. Believers are called to trust that God is working all things together for good (Romans 8:28), even when it seems time has been lost.

Renewed Purpose and Vision: When God restores lost time; it often comes with a renewed sense of purpose and vision. Believers who have wasted time can find new direction and motivation as God restores what was lost. This might involve stepping into new ministries, pursuing long-neglected dreams, or simply living with a renewed sense of God's calling.

Living with Hope: Knowing God can restore lost time fills believers with hope. It encourages them to look forward with expectation rather than dwelling on the past with regret. This hope exists in the belief that God is a restorer and redeemer, capable of bringing beauty out of ashes and joy out of mourning.

Challenges and misconceptions

While the idea of God restoring lost time is comforting, addressing some challenges and misconceptions associated with this concept is essential. Some may interpret the restoration of lost time as a guarantee that they will receive exactly what they lost. However, God's restoration does not always mean a return to the way things were. Instead, it often involves a new beginning, a different path, or a fresh start. Restoration is about God's best for our future, not necessarily a duplication of the past. Believers may become discouraged if they do not see immediate restoration. God's timing is different from human timing, and restoration may happen gradually or in ways that are not immediately apparent. Patience and faith are required to trust in God's perfect timing.

While God can restore lost time, this does not negate the consequences of actions. Believers are still responsible for their choices, and some consequences may remain. However, even in these situations, God's grace can bring redemption and new opportunities. It is common to compare one's life journey with others, especially when feeling that time has been lost. This can lead to feelings of inadequacy or jealousy. However, each person's journey is unique, and God's restoration tailors to fit individual needs and purposes. Believers are encouraged to focus on their relationship with God and trust His plan.

The concept of God restoring lost time is a powerful and encouraging truth that speaks to the heart of the Christian faith. It reveals God's sovereignty, grace, and ability to redeem seemingly hopeless situations. Through biblical examples, theological reflection, and practical application, God reminds believers that no time is truly lost when placed in God's hands.

God's restoration of lost time is about returning to what was and moving forward into a future filled with renewed purpose, hope, and joy. It is an invitation to trust in God's timing, live intentionally, and embrace the new opportunities God provides. Ultimately, the restoration of lost time points to the greater truth of God's redemptive work in the world, where all things will be made new in His perfect

As George and Cathy sat together reflecting on their journey, their conversation turned to the years they felt they wasted—seasons of missed opportunities, poor decisions, and times when they drifted from God's purpose. Tinged with regret but hope, Cathy shared how she had recently encountered the verse in **Joel 2:25**, where God promises to restore the years the locusts had eaten. "I believe that even the times we think are lost aren't wasted in God's hands," she said. George nodded in agreement, recalling moments when he felt his efforts were fruitless, only to see later how God had used those experiences to teach him patience and humility. "It's amazing," George said, "how God can take what we see as wasted time and weave it into His greater plan, bringing beauty and meaning out of what we thought was broken."

George sat on the edge of his couch, his hands clasped as he reflected on the conversation he had just had with Richard and Latasha. Their words lingered in his mind, stirring memories of a time in his life he had long considered wasted. He glanced at Susan, who was sitting across from him, her eyes filled with curiosity.

"You know," George began, his voice thoughtful, "listening to Richard talk about God's guidance got me thinking about something I've carried with me for years. For the longest time, I thought there was a period in my life that was just... wasted. But now I'm starting to see it differently."

Susan leaned forward, her attention fully on him. "What do you mean, George? What period?"

He sighed, a mixture of vulnerability and hope in his expression. "It was the years after I lost that job at the firm. I thought I had failed. I felt like I had wasted so much time trying to climb the ladder, and when it all came crashing down, I did not know who I was or what to do next. I spent months questioning everything—my decisions, my worth, even my faith. It felt like such a dark and pointless chapter."

Susan nodded, remembering how difficult those years had been for him. "But you came out of it, George. You found your footing again."

"That's the thing," George said, his voice soft but steady. "At the time, I thought I was just surviving, just trying to get through each day. However, looking back, I can see how God was at work, even when I could not see it. During those months of uncertainty, I spent more time in prayer and Scripture than I ever had before. I was not looking for answers about a career—I was just trying to find peace. And in that process, God began to reshape me."

Susan tilted her head, her eyes filled with understanding. "So, it wasn't wasted time?"

George shook his head. "Not at all. Losing that job forced me to slow down, to reevaluate what really mattered. I started volunteering at the community center during that time, just to keep myself busy. However, it was there that I discovered my passion for mentoring young people. I never would have found that if I had not been forced out of my comfort zone. And more than that, God was using that time to build my character—to teach me patience, humility, and trust."

He paused, a smile forming on his lips. "It's like that verse in Romans 8:28, where Paul says, 'And we know that in all things God works for the good of those who love Him, who have been called according to His purpose.' At the time, I thought everything was falling apart, but God was weaving it into something greater. That so-called 'wasted time' became the foundation for the work I do now—the work I truly love."

Susan reached over and placed a hand on his. "It's amazing how God does that, isn't it? Taking what feels broken and turning it into something beautiful."

George nodded his eyes misty with gratitude. "It is. In addition, it is a reminder that nothing is ever truly wasted with God. Even the seasons of waiting, of struggle, of uncertainty—they are all part of His plan. He is always working, even when we cannot see it. Now, whenever I face something difficult, I try to remember that. God's not finished with the story yet."

Susan smiled warmly. "You've come a long way, George. And your story—it's going to inspire so many others to trust God's timing."

George leaned back, a deep sense of peace settling over him. For the first time, he fully understood that every moment, even the ones that seemed broken, had been woven into God's greater plan. In addition, that realization filled him with hope for whatever lay ahead.

In every moment of life, even those that seem broken or purposeless, God is quietly at work, weaving them into the intricate tapestry of His greater plan. When we face struggles, setbacks, or seasons of waiting, it is easy to believe, those moments are wasted or devoid of meaning. Yet, the Bible reminds us that God can use all things for good (Romans 8:28). What looks like a detour to us is often God rerouting us to a path that aligns with His divine purpose. The broken pieces of our lives—the disappointments, the failures, the pain—are not discarded but reshaped and repurposed to reflect His glory and to fulfill His plan for us.

These moments teach us lessons we may not have learned otherwise. They build resilience, deepen our faith, and remind us of our dependence on God. When we look back, we often see how He used those seemingly wasted times to prepare us for something greater, shaping our character and clarifying our purpose. The broken seasons become a testimony of God's faithfulness and a source of encouragement to others. They reveal that nothing is ever truly lost or meaningless when surrendered to Him. Instead, every moment is a thread in the beautiful design He is weaving—a design that will only be fully revealed in His perfect timing.

CHAPTER 15

Unlock Your Limitations

As the door closed behind Richard and Susan, George stood for a moment in the quiet of his living room. The day's conversations replayed in his mind like echoes, each one carrying a weight he could not ignore. Susan had already gone to bed, but George felt an unusual pull to stay up, to sit with the thoughts stirring within him. He settled into his favorite chair, the dim light of the lamp casting soft shadows across the room, and let out a long, thoughtful sigh.

"Revelations for the soul," he murmured to himself. The phrase hung in the air like a question, challenging him to go deeper. He thought back to Richard's words about the secret place, how God speaks when we quiet ourselves and listen. He remembered his own reflections on how God weaves broken moments into His greater plan. Each revelation felt profound, yet George could not shake the feeling that there was more—something just beyond his current understanding.

He leaned forward, resting his elbows on his knees, and stared into the faint glow of the room. "What's holding me back?" he wondered aloud. He realized that while he had moments of clarity and insight, he often allowed the demands of life to crowd out the stillness he needed to truly hear from God. His busyness, doubts, and even his self-imposed limits on how God could work through him acted like walls, keeping him from fully embracing what God wanted to reveal.

"Maybe unlocking these limitations means surrendering them entirely," George thought. "I've been so focused on what I can understand or do, but maybe the key is to let go of my own reasoning and trust God to lead me beyond it." He closed his eyes and whispered a prayer, asking God to help him step into deeper trust, to show him how to let go of his constraints and allow divine wisdom to shape his soul.

As he sat there in the stillness, a sense of peace began to settle over him. George knew that the journey to understanding God's revelations was not about striving harder but about resting more fully in God's presence. It was about allowing God to reshape his mind, renew his heart, and guide him past the limits he had placed on himself. With that thought, George resolved to create more space for the secret place, to prioritize listening over speaking, and to trust that God would meet him there and take him further than he could imagine.

Unlocking your limitations is a powerful concept that resonates with many people, particularly those who feel constrained by circumstances, fear, doubt, or past experiences. The Bible offers profound wisdom on overcoming these limitations, providing encouragement and practical guidance on living a life free from the chains of self-imposed or externally imposed boundaries. In this essay, we will explore how biblical scriptures can unlock limitations, covering topics such as identity in Christ, the power of faith, the importance of renewing the mind, and the role of the Holy Spirit.

Before diving into how the Bible helps us overcome limitations, it is essential to understand them. We can define limitations as obstacles or barriers that prevent us from reaching our full potential. They can manifest in various forms—mental, emotional, physical, or spiritual—and often stem from:

Fear and Doubt: Fear of failure, rejection, or the unknown can create significant barriers. Doubt in one's abilities or God's promises can limit a person's willingness to step out in faith.

Adverse Experiences: Past failures, disappointments, or traumas can lead to a mindset of limitation, where individuals feel trapped by their previous experiences.

External Circumstances: Economic, social, or environmental factors can also impose limitations. For example, a lack of resources or opportunities can make it difficult to achieve specific goals.

Sin and Spiritual Bondage: Sin can create spiritual barriers, leading to guilt, shame, and separation from God. Spiritual bondage, whether through negative thought patterns or demonic influence, can also limit a person's freedom and growth.

Cultural and Societal Norms: Sometimes, cultural or societal expectations can create limitations, dictating what is possible or acceptable based on factors like gender, race, or social status.

How to overcoming limitations.

One of the most powerful truths in the Bible is the believer's identity in Christ. Understanding who you are in Christ is the foundation for overcoming limitations, as it shifts your perspective from focusing on your weaknesses to embracing your God-given strengths. 2 Corinthians 5:17 declares, "Therefore if anyone is in Christ, he is a new creation. The old has passed away; behold, the new has come." This scripture emphasizes that your past does not define you. In Christ, you have a new identity, and your old limitations no longer have power over you. **Romans 8:37** states, "No, in all these things we are more than conquerors through him who loved us." This verse encourages believers that they are not just survivors but victors through Christ. Whatever limitations you face, you can overcome them through the strength that comes from Christ. **Galatians 3:26** affirms, "For in Christ Jesus you are all sons of God, through faith." Recognizing that you are a child of God, loved and valued by Him, can break the chains of limitations imposed by feelings of inadequacy or worthlessness. **1 Corinthians 2:16** reveals, "But we have the mind of Christ." This scripture means you can access divine wisdom and insight as a believer. You are not limited by human understanding; you can tap into the mind of Christ to navigate challenges and limitations.

The power of faith: moving Mountains.

Faith is a central theme in the Bible and is crucial for unlocking limitations. Faith is not just belief in God; it is trust in His promises and power, even when circumstances seem impossible.

Faith as Small as a Mustard Seed: In **Matthew 17:20**, Jesus tells His disciples, "Truly I tell you, if you have faith as small as a mustard seed, you can say to this mountain, 'Move from here to there,' and it will move. Nothing will be impossible for you." This verse highlights that even the smallest amount of faith can overcome the most significant obstacles. It is a reminder that limitations are not as powerful as the faith you place in God.

Walking by Faith, Not by Sight: **2 Corinthians 5:7** instructs, "For we walk by faith, not by sight." This scripture challenges believers to look beyond their immediate circumstances and trust God's unseen work. Often, limitations are what we see or experience, but faith calls us to trust God's excellent plan.

Faith without Works are dead: James 2:17 reminds us, "So also faith by itself if it does not have works, is dead." Unlocking limitations requires active faith—faith that is demonstrated through actions. Believing in God's promises should propel you to step out, take risks, and pursue what seems impossible.

The Shield of Faith: **Ephesians 6:16** speaks of "the shield of faith, with which you can extinguish all the flaming arrows of the evil one." This verse emphasizes faith as a protective measure against spiritual attacks, doubts, and fears that seek to reinforce limitations.

Renewing the mind: Transforming thought patterns.

Many limitations are rooted in the mind—negative thought patterns, false beliefs, and limiting perceptions. The Bible places significant emphasis on the renewal of the mind as a key to transformation and freedom from limitations. **Romans 12:2** encourages believers, "Do not conform to the pattern of this world but be transformed by renewing your mind. Then you can test and approve God's will—his good, pleasing, and perfect will." This verse indicates that breaking free from limitations requires a change in thinking. Renewing your mind with God's truth allows you to see beyond the limitations that the world imposes.

We must take every thought captive: **2 Corinthians 10:5** instructs, "We demolish arguments and every pretension that sets itself up against the knowledge of God, and we take captive every thought to make it obedient to Christ." This scripture highlights the importance of controlling your thoughts. Limiting beliefs often stem from negative thoughts that contradict God's word. Taking these thoughts captive allows you to align your thinking with God's truth and overcome limitations. We must set our minds on the things above. **Colossians 3:2** says, "Set your minds on things above, not earthly things." This verse encourages believers to focus on eternal, divine realities rather than temporary, earthly limitations. By setting your mind on God's purposes and promises, you can transcend the constraints imposed by earthly circumstances. We must think about whatever is true. **Philippians 4:8** advises, "Finally, brothers and sisters, whatever is true, whatever is noble, whatever is right, whatever is pure, whatever is lovely, whatever is admirable—if anything is excellent or praiseworthy—think about such things." This verse underscores the power of positive thinking and focusing on God's goodness. Positive, faith-filled thinking can break the cycle of limitation and open up new possibilities.

The Holy Spirit empowers and guides us.

The Holy Spirit plays a crucial role in unlocking limitations. As the third person of the Trinity, the Holy Spirit empowers, guides, and equips believers to overcome obstacles and live in freedom.

The Holy Spirit grants us the spirit of power, love, and a sound mind. 2 Timothy 1:7 declares, "For God has not given us a spirit of fear but of power and love and a sound mind." This verse reminds believers that fear—one of the most common sources of limitation—does not come from God. Instead, the Holy Spirit provides the power, love, and sound mind to overcome fear and other limitations. We should always be mindful to allow the Holy Spirit to lead us. **Romans 8:14** states, "For those whom the Spirit of God leads are the children of God." Being led by the Holy Spirit is when your limitations or understanding does not bind you. The Holy Spirit guides you into God's perfect will, often leading you to places and opportunities you never thought possible.

The Gifts of the Spirit: **1 Corinthians 12** discusses the gifts of the Spirit—wisdom, knowledge, faith, healing, miracles, prophecy, discernment, tongues, and tongue interpretation. God grants these gifts to believers to overcome limitations in ministry and life. For example, the gift of wisdom can help you navigate complex situations that seem limiting, while the gift of faith can empower you to believe in the impossible.

The Fruit of the Spirit: **Galatians 5:22-23** describes the fruit of the Spirit—love, joy, peace, patience, kindness, goodness, faithfulness, gentleness, and self-control. These attributes are essential for overcoming limitations, as they reflect the character of Christ in a believer's life. For instance, patience can help you endure and overcome long-standing limitations, while self-control can prevent you from falling into habits that reinforce limitations.

Practical steps to unlocking limitations with Scripture.

The Bible provides theological insights and practical steps for overcoming limitations. Applying these scriptures to your life involves intentional action and commitment. **Identify Your Limitations**: The first step to overcoming limitations is identifying them. Pray for discernment to understand what is holding you back. Is it fear, doubt, a negative experience, or something else? Once you identify the limitation, you can address it with specific scriptures.

Speak the Word of God: **Proverbs 18:21** says, "Death and life are in the power of the tongue." Speaking God's word over your life is a powerful way to unlock limitations

George and Richard was sitting in one of their favorite places to get away. Their wives were out shopping as usual. While they discussed their lesson learned to date, Minister James Thompkins cane to their table. As they begin to explain to Minster Thompkins heir revelation recent months, their faces show the stress of increased understanding. Minister Thompkins relieved by asking one simple question – who is stopping you,.

CHAPTER 16

WHAT'S STOPPING YOU

The question "What's stopping you?" resonates deeply with individuals across all walks of life. It speaks to the barriers, real or perceived, that hold us back from achieving our fullest potential, realizing our dreams, or even just taking the next step in life. These barriers can be physical, emotional, mental, or spiritual, and they often work in complex ways that can be difficult to untangle.

The essence of this question lies in self-reflection and the search for understanding. It is not merely about identifying external obstacles but also about uncovering internal ones. By asking this question; we challenge ourselves to confront the limitations we face—whether they are rooted in fear, doubt, past experiences, societal expectations, or spiritual disconnection—and seek ways to overcome them.

The mind is a powerful tool capable of profoundly shaping our reality. However, it can also be a significant source of limitation. Psychological barriers often manifest as self-doubt, limiting beliefs, or negative thought patterns that prevent us from moving forward. One of the most common psychological barriers is self-doubt, deeply intertwined with low self-esteem. We hesitate to take risks or pursue opportunities when we are confident in our abilities and worth. This doubt can stem from past failures, negative feedback, or a lack of confidence. It creates a mindset that says, "I'm not good enough," "I can't do this," or "I don't deserve success." Limiting beliefs are deeply ingrained convictions about the world around us. These beliefs often go unnoticed, operating beneath the surface to shape our decisions and behaviors. For example, someone may believe that success is only for the lucky or that we must always play it safe to avoid failure. These beliefs can be self-fulfilling prophecies, limiting what we believe is possible and, consequently, what we achieve.

We must rid ourselves of negative thought patterns. The way we think can either propel us forward or hold us back. Negative thought patterns, such as catastrophizing (expecting the worst), overgeneralizing (believing one failure means future failures), or all-or-nothing thinking (seeing things in black and white), can paralyze us. These patterns create mental roadblocks that prevent us from taking action or seeing possibilities.

Fear is one of the most potent forces that can stop us from achieving our goals. It manifests in various forms, including fear of failure, rejection, the unknown, and success.

Fear of Failure: The fear of failure is the most pervasive form of fear. It is the anxiety that comes with the possibility of not meeting expectations, whether they are our own or those of others. This fear can lead to avoidance behaviors, where we procrastinate, make excuses, or abandon our goals altogether to avoid the pain of failing.

Fear of Rejection: For many, rejection is tied to the need for acceptance and validation from others. This fear can prevent us from putting ourselves out there—whether it is applying for a job, pursuing a relationship, or sharing our creative work. The potential of being judged, criticized, or dismissed can be paralyzing.

Fear of the Unknown: Uncertainty is a natural part of life, but for some, the fear of the unknown can be debilitating. This fear arises when we step outside our comfort zones, face new challenges, or venture into uncharted territory. The unpredictability of outcomes can cause us to cling to the familiar, even if it limits our growth.

Fear of Success: While it may seem counterintuitive, the fear of success is real. It stems from the anxiety about the changes and responsibilities that success may bring. This fear can manifest as self-sabotage, where we unconsciously undermine our efforts to avoid the pressures or expectations that come with success.

Procrastination is a common issue that can stop us from reaching our goals. It delays or postpones tasks, often due to a lack of motivation, fear of failure, or overwhelm. Procrastination can be a form of self-sabotage, where we avoid crucial tasks for our progress. Procrastination often provides temporary relief from the discomfort of complex tasks. By putting off a task, we avoid the stress, anxiety, or effort associated with it. However, this delay comes at a cost—lost time, missed opportunities, and increased stress as deadlines approach. Overwhelming occurs when a task is too large, complex, or daunting. This can lead to paralysis, where we do not know where to start, so we do not start at all. On the other hand, perfectionism is the unrealistic expectation that we must perform perfectly or not at all. This mindset can cause us to delay tasks out of fear that we will not meet our high standards. Procrastination can take hold when we lack clarity about our goals or do not effectively prioritize tasks. Putting off important tasks instead of more immediate, less important ones is easy without a clear plan or a sense of urgency.

Societal pressures and expectations can also act as significant barriers to our progress. These pressures come from various sources—family, culture, peers, and the media—and can influence our choices, behaviors, and beliefs. Every society has its own norms and expectations that dictate what it considers acceptable or successful. These norms can create pressure to conform, even when it goes against our desires or potential.

Peer pressure can lead to decisions not in our best interest, driven by the need for acceptance or fear of standing out. This pressure can prevent us from taking risks or pursuing goals that do not align with the group.

For example, societal expectations about career paths, gender roles, or lifestyle choices can limit our freedom to pursue what we want. The influence of peers can be both positive and negative. On the negative side, peer pressure can lead to decisions not in our best interest, driven by the need for acceptance or fear of standing out. This pressure can prevent us from taking risks or pursuing goals that do not align with the group. Family can be a source of support and encouragement, but it can also be a source of pressure. Expectations from parents or relatives regarding career choices, marriage, or lifestyle can create internal conflict, where we feel torn between meeting their expectations and following our path. The media, particularly social media, significantly shapes our perceptions of success and worth. The constant comparison to others' curated lives can create feelings of inadequacy, leading to self-doubt and limiting beliefs. The pressure to "keep up" can cause us to pursue goals that are not indeed our own, stopping us from living authentically.

The pressure to "keep up" with societal expectations, cultural trends, or the achievements of others can be an overwhelming force, driving us to pursue goals that do not truly align with who we are. In a world dominated by comparisons—often fueled by social media and societal norms—it is easy to measure our success by external benchmarks. We chase careers, accolades, or lifestyles that look impressive to others but fail to resonate with our deepest values and desires. Over time, this misalignment creates a sense of emptiness, as our efforts to keep up with others pull us further away from our authentic selves.

This pursuit of external validation can lead to exhaustion, frustration, and a loss of identity. When our actions are dictated by the desire to meet others' expectations rather than our own convictions, we sacrifice the freedom to live authentically. Instead of discovering our unique path, we may find ourselves trapped in cycles of striving, always working toward goals that do not bring fulfillment. The joy of pursuing a purpose rooted in our individuality is replaced by the anxiety of keeping pace with standards we never chose for ourselves.

Living authentically requires courage and intentionality. It means stepping back from the noise of comparison and asking, "What truly matters to me?" It involves distinguishing between what we value and what we have been told to value. This process is not always easy; it may require breaking away from societal norms or redefining success on our terms. However, the reward is profound: a life that reflects our true selves, grounded in purpose, joy, and integrity. By letting go of the pressure to keep up, we free ourselves to embrace our unique journey—a path that leads to lasting fulfillment and a deeper connection to our own hearts and to those around us.

We limit our soul.

Spiritual disconnection can be a profound barrier to personal growth and fulfillment. When disconnected from our spiritual source—God, a higher power, or our inner self—we may feel lost, purposeless, or unfulfilled. A sense of purpose is essential for motivation and direction. When spiritually disconnected, we may struggle to find meaning in our actions or understand our place in the world. This lack of purpose can lead to stagnation, where we drift aimlessly or pursue goals that do not align with our true calling. Spiritual disconnection can also manifest as feelings of guilt or shame, particularly if we feel that we have strayed from our beliefs or values. These feelings can be paralyzing, preventing us from moving forward or seeking forgiveness and restoration.

The lack of faith causes us to struggle. Faith is the belief in something greater than you are. Whether it is a higher power, a divine plan, or the goodness of life, we may struggle with doubt, fear, and hopelessness when we lack faith. This lack of faith can stop us from taking bold steps or trusting that things will work out. Inner peace is a state of mental and emotional calmness rooted in spiritual connection. We feel anxious, restless, or without this kind of peace. This mindset hinders our decision-making, taking risks, or moving forward. We must break free. Understanding what stops us is the first step; the next step is overcoming these barriers. Here, we will explore strategies for breaking free from the limitations that hold us back.

Self-awareness is the foundation of personal growth. It involves understanding your thoughts, emotions, behaviors, and underlying beliefs and motivations that drive them. By becoming more self-aware, you can identify the barriers that stop you and take steps to overcome them. Two valuable methods to improve self-awareness are journaling and mindfulness.

Journaling: Writing down your thoughts and feelings can help clarify what stops you. Journaling allows you to reflect on your experiences, identify patterns, and explore your emotions in a safe and non-judgmental space.

Mindfulness and Meditation: Mindfulness practices, such as meditation, can help you become more aware of your thoughts and feelings in the present moment. This awareness allows us to continue generating self-awareness. Bottom of Form

Minister Thompkins sat across from George and Richard, his tone compassionate yet firm as he began addressing a truth many overlook. "Often, the biggest obstacles in our lives aren't external—they're within us," he said, meeting their eyes. He explained that people hinder themselves through doubt, fear, and a reluctance to trust God's plan. "We allow negative self-talk, past failures, and a fear of the unknown to hold us back," he continued. "Instead of stepping out in faith, we second-guess ourselves and sometimes even question God's promises." Minister Thompkins pointed out that while challenges will always exist, the real battle often lies in our mindset and willingness to surrender control.

As the conversation deepened, Minister Thompkins shared examples from Scripture, reminding George and Richard of how people like Moses and Gideon initially doubted their ability to fulfill God's call. "God equips those He calls, but it's up to us to stop sabotaging ourselves with excuses and to step into the opportunities He provides," he said passionately. He encouraged them to recognize how they might be holding themselves back—whether through procrastination, pride, or a lack of discipline—and commit to breaking free from those patterns. "When we align our thoughts and actions with God's truth, we remove the barriers we've placed in our path," Minister Thompkins concluded. His words left George and Richard challenged and inspired, eager to reflect on their lives and move forward in faith.

CHAPTER 17

FINDING GOD IN HIDDEN PLACES

The search for God is a journey many embark on to understand the divine in a world filled with distractions and challenges. While some find God in the grand and prominent—places of worship, sacred texts, or miraculous events—others discover Him in life's hidden and subtle corners. These "hidden places" that we often overlook but are rich with divine presence, offering profound spiritual insights and deepening our relationship with the Creator. This essay explores finding God in hidden places, drawing on biblical scriptures and spiritual reflections to illuminate how God reveals His presence in the unseen, the ordinary, and the unexpected.

The Bible is deeply rooted in the idea that we can find God in hidden places. God's hiddenness does not imply absence but rather a different mode of presence—one that invites seekers to look beyond the surface and engage with the mystery of the divine. Scripture often speaks of God as hidden, yet this hiddenness is not about God being distant or unreachable. Instead, it is an invitation to seek Him sincerely and openly. **Isaiah 45:15** states, "Truly, you are a God who hides himself, O God of Israel, the Savior." This verse acknowledges the paradox of a hidden and revealed God, challenging believers to look deeper and trust His presence, even when it is not immediately apparent.

One of the profound truths of the Christian faith is that God is present in life's ordinary and everyday moments. The Bible inspires us with stories where God meets people in mundane settings—a shepherd's field, a quiet garden, a humble home. In **1 Kings 19:11-12,** Elijah encounters God not in the wind, earthquake, or fire but in a "still small voice." This passage reminds us that God's presence often comes in subtle, quiet ways, requiring us to be attentive and receptive.

The ultimate example of God in hidden places is the incarnation of Jesus Christ. God chose to reveal Himself not through a display of overwhelming power but through the humble birth of a child in a manger. **Philippians 2:6-7** describes how Jesus, "being in very nature God, did not consider equality with God something to be used to his advantage; rather, he made himself nothing by taking the very nature of a servant, being made in human likeness." The incarnation teaches us that God can be found in the most unexpected and humble places, emphasizing the value of the ordinary and the overlooked.

One of the most accessible hidden places where God reveals Himself is in nature. With its beauty, complexity, and order, the natural world reflects the Creator's hand, offering a silent testimony to His presence. **The Heavens Declare the Glory of God**: **Psalm 19:1** states, "The heavens declare the glory of God; the skies proclaim the work of his hands." This verse reminds us that the natural world is a canvas displaying God's glory. From the vastness of the stars to the intricacy of a flower, nature is a place where God's presence is revealed to those who take the time to observe and reflect. **God's Provision in the Natural World**: Jesus often used nature to illustrate spiritual truths. In **Matthew 6:26,** He says, "Look at the birds of the air; they do not sow or reap or store away in barns, and yet your heavenly Father feeds them. Are you not much more valuable than they?"

Here, Jesus points to the natural world as a testament to God's care and provision, encouraging believers to trust His unseen but ever-present hand.

The Stillness of Creation: Nature also teaches us the importance of stillness and quiet in finding God. **Psalm 46:10** urges, "Be still, and know that I am God." In the stillness of a forest, the calm of a sunrise, or the gentle flow of a river, we can find a sense of peace and awareness of God's presence in the busyness of life. **Finding God in Solitude and Silence.** In a world filled with noise and constant activity, solitude and silence are usually where we feel God's presence. The Bible encourages us to seek out these quiet moments to connect with God deeper.

Jesus in Solitude: Throughout His ministry, Jesus often withdrew to solitary places to pray and commune with the Father. **Mark 1:35** recounts, "Very early in the morning, while it was still dark, Jesus got up, left the house, and went off to a solitary place, where he prayed." This practice of seeking solitude shows that even Jesus found it necessary to step away from the crowds and noise to be alone with God, emphasizing the importance of solitude in spiritual life.

The power of silence.

Silence is a powerful tool for spiritual growth, allowing us to hear God's "still small voice." In **Habakkuk 2:20,** we read, "But the Lord is in his holy temple; let all the earth be silent before him." Silence before God is not just the absence of noise but also an active posture of listening and reverence, creating space for God to speak to our hearts. The early Christian monastic tradition, particularly the Desert Fathers, emphasized finding God in the silence and solitude of the desert. These spiritual pioneers sought to escape the world's distractions to encounter God in quiet and barren places. Their lives and teachings remind us that the hidden places, whether literal deserts or our hearts' inner deserts are fertile ground for experiencing God's presence.

Finding God in suffering and trials.

Another hidden place where God hides is in suffering and trials. While it may seem paradoxical, the Bible teaches that God is incredibly close to the brokenhearted and the suffering. **God's Presence in Suffering**: Psalm 34:18 offers comfort with the words, "The Lord is close to the brokenhearted and saves those who are crushed in spirit." This verse assures us that in our moments of deepest pain. God is not distant but near, offering comfort and strength. We often encounter God most profoundly in our dark and hidden places.

The Refiner's Fire: The imagery of the refiner's fire used in Scripture to describe how God uses trials to purify and strengthen our faith. In **Malachi 3:3,** we read, "He will sit as a refiner and purifier of silver; he will purify the Levites and refine them like gold and silver." Just as precious metals are refined through fire, our faith and character are refined through trials. These problematic experiences, though painful, can become places where we encounter God's transformative work in our lives.

Paul's Thorn in the Flesh: The Apostle Paul's experience of suffering offers a powerful example of finding God's strength in weakness. In 2 Corinthians 12:9-10, Paul writes, "But he said to me, 'My grace is sufficient for you, for my power is made perfect in weakness.' Therefore, I will boast all the more gladly about my weaknesses so that Christ's power may rest on me." Paul's "thorn in the flesh" was a source of suffering, yet he profoundly experienced God's grace and power. This passage teaches us that our weaknesses and struggles can be hidden places where God's presence and power are most evident.

Finding God in community and relationships.

While solitude and silence are essential for spiritual growth, God also reveals Himself in the hidden places of community and relationships. The Bible emphasizes the importance of fellowship. God uses others to manifest His presence. The New Testament describes the church as the "body of Christ," with each member playing a vital role in the community's life. In **1 Corinthians 12:12-27**, Paul explains that just as a body has many parts, each with different functions, the church is also made up of diverse individuals, each contributing to the whole. This metaphor highlights how God is present in the relationships and interactions between believers, working through them to support, encourage, and build each other up. Jesus made a powerful promise regarding His presence in the community in **Matthew 18:20:** "For where two or three gather in my name, there am I with them." This verse underscores the idea that God is present in the fellowship of believers. When we come together in His name, whether in worship, prayer, or service, we create a space where God is uniquely present and active. The practice of hospitality is another way in which God reveals Himself in hidden places. Hebrews 13:2 advises, "Do not forget to show hospitality to strangers, for by so doing some people have shown hospitality to angels without knowing it." This verse suggests that in opening our homes and lives to other people; we may unknowingly encounter God's presence. Acts of kindness and hospitality become sacred moments where God is at work, often in unseen ways. God's heart for the marginalized and the poor is a central theme in the Bible, usually in these hidden places. God's presence is most powerfully revealed among the least and the lost. In **Matthew 25:40**, Jesus teaches, "Truly I tell you, whatever you did for one of the least of these brothers and sisters of mine.

When George and Richard returned to George's home, Susan and Cathy were busy cooking. "What do you two have to tell us? "We know you both had the mountaintop experience and witnessed a burning bush. George and Richard sat across from Susan and Cathy, their faces glowing excitedly as they shared their recent revelation about God's presence. "You know," George began, "we've always heard about seeking God, but we never realized how often He hides in the ordinary and unexpected places in our lives." He explained how they had been reflecting on moments when they felt alone or uncertain, only to see later how God had worked behind the scenes. "Sometimes it's in the quiet moments, like the stillness of a sunrise or the comforting words of a friend. Other times, it's in the struggles where He's teaching us resilience and trust," George added.

Richard nodded, picking up where George left off. "We also realized that God often hides in the opportunities we overlook or the people we dismiss. It's like He's waiting for us to slow down, open our hearts, and truly seek Him," he said. Richard shared how a recent conversation with a stranger had unexpectedly given him clarity about a tough decision, making him realize God had been speaking through that person. "It's humbling to think that God is always there, but we miss Him because we're looking in the wrong places," he concluded. Susan and Cathy listened intently, inspired by their words and encouraged to look for God in every aspect of their lives.

As they sat together, George leaned forward, his voice steady and thoughtful. "You know," he began, looking at Susan, Richard, and Cathy, "I've been thinking about how we often let the world around us dictate how we live—our moods, choices, even our sense of worth. But I've realized we're meant to live from the inside out, not the outside." He paused, letting his words sink in. "When we live from the inside out, we draw strength from the Spirit of God within us.

As Christians, God calls us to live a life rooted in God's truth, not dictated by the ever-changing standards and pressures of the world around us. When we allow the world to influence our moods, choices, and sense of worth, we risk building our identity on a foundation that is fragile and unstable. Society often promotes superficial values—success measured by wealth, beauty, or social status—which can leave us feeling inadequate or unfulfilled. However, God's Word reminds us that our worth comes from Him alone. Ephesians 2:10 declares that we are His workmanship, created for good works in Christ. Our value is not tied to external achievements or opinions but to the unchanging love of our Creator.

God desires for us to live with a sense of purpose and freedom, unshackled by the world's expectations. Romans 12:2 exhorts us not to conform to the patterns of this world but to be transformed by the renewing of our minds so that we may discern God has will—His good, pleasing, and perfect will. This transformation happens when we shift our focus from external influences to God's eternal truth. By anchoring our identity and choices in Him, we can live confidently and authentically, free from the anxiety of trying to meet worldly standards. God's plan is for us to find our worth in His love, to make decisions based on His guidance, and to live as reflections of His grace and light in a world desperately in need of His truth.

CHAPTER 18

LIVING FROM THE INSIDE OUT

Living from the inside out is a profound and transformative concept that invites individuals to align their outer lives with their inner values, beliefs, and spiritual truths. This way of living contrasts with an outside-in approach, where external circumstances, societal expectations, or material pursuits dictate one's sense of identity, purpose, and direction. The Bible offers extensive guidance on this topic, encouraging believers to cultivate an inner life grounded in God's truth, which then informs and shapes their actions, relationships, and decisions.

We must seek to explore the biblical foundations of living from the inside out, examining key scriptures that illuminate this path. We will also discuss practical ways to cultivate an inner life that reflects God's presence and guidance and how this approach can lead to a life of integrity, peace, and spiritual fulfillment. The Bible emphasizes the importance of the inner life—the heart, mind, and soul—as the wellspring from which all actions flow. This concept is central to understanding how to live from the inside out, as it emphasizes nurturing a relationship with God and allowing that relationship to transform every aspect of life.

Proverbs 4:23 declares, "Above all else, guard your heart, for everything you do flows from it." This verse highlights the importance of the heart as the source of all our actions and decisions. In biblical terms, the heart represents the core of our being—our thoughts, emotions, desires, and will. Living from the inside out means guarding and cultivating our hearts, ensuring they align with God's truth and love.

Romans 12:2 urges believers, "Do not conform to the pattern of this world but be transformed by renewing your mind. Then you can test and approve God's will—his good, pleasing, and perfect will." This scripture underscores the importance of inner transformation, beginning with the mind. By renewing our minds with God's word and truth, we are empowered to live in a way that reflects His will rather than letting external influences shape us.

The New Testament teaches believers that they are temples of the Holy Spirit, who dwell within them. In **1 Corinthians 6:19-20**, Paul writes, "Do you not know that your bodies are temples of the Holy Spirit, who is in you, whom you have received from God? You are not your own; you were bought at a price. Therefore, honor God with your bodies." This indwelling presence of the Holy Spirit is not just a fact but a transformative power that guides, empowers, and changes us from within, giving us hope and inspiration.

Living from the inside out begins with cultivating an inner life deeply connected to God. This involves developing a heart responsive to God's leading, a mind renewed by His truth, and a soul nourished by His presence. Integrity is about living in alignment with one's values and beliefs; for Christians, this means living in alignment with God's word. **Psalm 51:10** expresses the desire for inner purity: "Create in me a pure heart, O God, and renew a steadfast spirit within me." A heart of integrity is undivided and wholly devoted to God, leading to actions consistent with His will.

Meditation and prayer are not just vital practices for nurturing the inner life but powerful tools that shape our thoughts, attitudes, and actions. **Psalm 1:2-3** describes the blessed person as one whose "delight is in the law of the Lord and meditates on his law day and night. That person is like a tree planted by streams of water, which yields its fruit in season and whose leaf does not wither—whatever they do prospers." By meditating on God's word and praying, we cultivate a deep connection that empowers us to align our lives with His will.

Gratitude is an assertive attitude that transforms our inner life. **Philippians 4:6-7** encourages believers, "Do not be anxious about anything, but in every situation, by prayer and petition, with thanksgiving, present your requests to God. And the peace of God, which transcends all understanding, will guard your hearts and minds in Christ Jesus." A heart filled with gratitude focused on God's goodness, leading to peace and contentment flowing into every life area.

Once the inner life is cultivated and aligned with God's truth, it naturally influences the outer life—our actions, decisions, relationships, and interactions with the world. Living from the inside out means allowing the inner work of God in our hearts to manifest in how we live each day. Integrity is not about what we believe but about how we live. **James 2:17** states, "In the same way, faith by itself, if it is not accompanied by action, is dead." Living from the inside out requires that our actions be consistent with our faith and beliefs. This means acting with honesty, kindness, and justice in all our dealings, reflecting the character of Christ in the world.

We must serve others with a pure heart: Service is a central aspect of the Christian life, but we must have the right motives. In **Matthew 6:1-4**, Jesus warns against performing righteous acts for the sake of being seen by others, urging instead that our service be done in secret, with a pure heart: "Then Your Father, who sees what is done in secret, will reward you." Living from the inside out means serving others with genuine love and compassion, not for recognition or personal gain. The outward expression of a life lived from the inside out is marked by love and forgiveness. **Colossians 3:12-14** instructs, "Therefore, as God's chosen people, holy and dearly loved, clothe yourselves with compassion, kindness, humility, gentleness, and patience. Bear with each other and forgive one another if any of you has a grievance against someone. Forgive as the Lord forgave you. And over all these virtues put on love, which binds them all together in perfect unity." Love and forgiveness are the fruits of a heart transformed by God's grace and the foundation of healthy relationships and community.

The challenge of living from the inside out in a world focused on living, looking out.

Living from the inside out can be challenging in a world that often prioritizes external success, appearances, and material wealth. Society's pressures can pull us away from our inner values and lead us to conform to worldly standards. However, the Bible offers wisdom and encouragement for staying true to this inner-outward approach to life. We should resist conformity to the world's way of doing things. Resisting Conformity to the World: **Romans 12:2** provides a clear directive: "Do not conform to the pattern of this world, but be transformed by the renewing of your mind." The world often promotes values contrary to God's will, such as selfishness, pride, and materialism. Living from the inside out requires resisting these pressures and allowing God's truth to shape our values and decisions.

The desire for approval and validation from others can be a significant obstacle to living from the inside out. Jesus addressed this issue in **Matthew 6:1-18**, where He cautions against performing religious acts for the sake of visibility to others. Instead, He encourages His followers to seek God's approval above all. **Galatians 1:10** echoes this sentiment: "Am I now trying to win the approval of human beings, or God? Alternatively, am I trying to please people? If I were still trying to please people, I would not be a servant of Christ." This scripture reminds us to prioritize God's approval over human praise, ensuring our actions are genuine faith rather than a desire for external validation.

Pursuing material wealth and success can lead us away from a life lived from the inside out. In **Matthew 6:19-21**, Jesus teaches, "Do not store up for yourselves treasures on earth, where moths and vermin destroy, and where thieves break in and steal. However, store up for yourselves treasures in heaven, where moths and vermin do not destroy, and where thieves do not break in and steal. For where your treasure is, there your heart will be also." This passage challenges us to consider where we place our ultimate value—on temporal, earthly things or eternal, spiritual realities.

The Rewards of living from the inside out.

While living from the inside out may present challenges, it also offers profound rewards. When our lives align with God's truth and our inner lives are cultivated in His presence, we experience a deep sense of peace, fulfillment, and purpose that transcends external circumstances.

One of the most significant rewards of living from the inside out is inner peace. **Philippians 4:6-7** speaks of the peace that comes from trusting in God: "Do not be anxious about anything, but in every situation, by prayer and petition, with thanksgiving, present your requests to God. And the peace of God, which transcends all understanding, will guard your hearts and minds in Christ Jesus." This peace is not dependent on external circumstances but is rooted in a deep relationship with God. Our lives are infused with purpose and meaning when we live from the inside out.

Susan and Cathy sat together, reflecting on George's words about living from the inside out. Susan was the first to speak, and her tone was thoughtful. "It really struck me when George said that we let the outside world dictate our peace and purpose," she admitted. "I've done that more times than I can count—letting someone's opinion or a bad day completely throw me off course." She paused, then added idea of drawing strength from the Spirit within us, from our relationship with God, which, makes so much sense. It's like having an anchor, something unshakable, no matter what storms come our way." Cathy nodded in agreement, feeling the same conviction. "I think I've been focusing too much on external validation," Susan continued. "But this reminds me that who I am in Christ should be enough."

Cathy smiled her voice soft but firm. "For me, it's about trust," she said. "Trusting what God has placed inside me is enough to face anything outside of me. When George talked about nurturing our inner relationship with God, it felt like a wake-up call. I've been so busy trying to fix everything around me that I've neglected what's most important." She sighed, then added, "Living from the inside out means we don't just react to life; we respond with God's strength and wisdom. That's powerful." The two women sat quietly for a moment, the weight of their discussion settling in. They both felt a renewed commitment to prioritize their inner spiritual growth and to live in a way that reflected God's peace and purpose. We have to come face to face with God.

Prioritizing inner spiritual growth is essential for living a life that reflects God's peace and purpose. In a world filled with distractions, challenges, and pressures, spiritual growth serves as the anchor that keeps us grounded in God's truth. It is through this growth that we develop a deeper understanding of who God is, who we are in Him, and the purpose He has for our lives. When we invest time in prayer, studying Scripture, and seeking God's presence, we align our hearts with His will and invite His transformative power into every aspect of our being. This inner transformation equips us to navigate life's ups and downs with a sense of peace that surpasses all understanding—a peace that can only come from a close relationship with God.

Living in a way that reflects God's peace and purpose is not only beneficial for our own well-being but also serves as a powerful testimony to those around us. When we prioritize our spiritual growth, our lives become a reflection of God's love, grace, and truth. In a world often marked by chaos and confusion, the peace of God evident in our actions and attitudes becomes a beacon of hope to others. It shows them that there is a deeper, eternal source of joy and purpose available to all who seek Him. Moreover, living in alignment with God's purpose allows us to fulfill the unique calling He has placed on our lives, using our gifts and experiences to serve Him and others. By prioritizing our inner spiritual growth, we not only experience the fullness of life that God intends for us but also become instruments of His peace and purpose in a world that desperately needs both.

When we prioritize spiritual growth and align our lives with God's purpose, we open ourselves to experiencing the fullness of life He intends for us. Jesus said, "I have come that they may have life, and have it to the full" (John 10:10). This fullness is not rooted in material wealth or worldly success but in a deep, abiding relationship with God. As we grow spiritually, we learn to trust Him more, find joy in His presence, and live with a sense of peace that surpasses understanding. This peace guards our hearts and minds, empowering us to face challenges without fear or anxiety. Through spiritual maturity, we begin to see life through God's perspective, finding purpose and meaning even in difficult circumstances.

Moreover, as we experience the transformative power of God's peace, we become vessels of that peace for others. The world is full with people searching for hope, healing, and purpose, and as Christians, we are called to be the light in the darkness. This means actively sharing God's love through our words and actions, being peacemakers in our communities, and living in a way that reflects His grace and truth. To do this, we must continually seek God's guidance through prayer, immerse ourselves in Scripture to gain wisdom, and cultivate humility and compassion in our interactions. By allowing God to work through us, we can affect the world around us, pointing others to the peace and purpose that can only be found in Him. It is not just; about what we receive from God but also about how we extend His blessings to that in need, fulfilling our role as His hands and feet in the world.

CHAPTER 19

TAKE ME TO THE KING

Coming face to face with God is one of the Bible's most profound and awe-inspiring themes. It represents a moment of deep spiritual encounter, where the divine presence reveals an undeniable and transformative way. Such encounters are not just about seeing God with physical eyes but involve an intimate experience of His presence, holiness, and overwhelming love. Throughout the Bible, numerous accounts of individuals had the extraordinary experience of coming face to face with God. These encounters reveal various aspects of God's nature—His holiness, glory, and intimate involvement in human affairs.

Moses and the Burning Bush: One of the most famous encounters with God is the story of Moses and the burning bush in **Exodus 3**. While tending his father-in-law's sheep, Moses comes across a bush on fire. God speaks to him when he approaches, saying, and "Do not come any closer. Take off your sandals, for where you stand is holy ground" **[Exodus 3:5]**. This encounter marks a turning point in Moses' life, as God called to lead the Israelites out of slavery in Egypt. Here, God emphasizes His holiness, and Moses' life is irrevocably changed as he faces the divine.

Jacob Wrestling with God: Another significant biblical account of coming face to face with God in **Genesis 32:22-32**, where Jacob wrestles with a mysterious man through the night. This man was God Himself. After the struggle, Jacob declares, "It is because I saw God face to face, and yet my life was spared" **[Genesis 32:30]**. This encounter changes Jacob's name to Israel and symbolizes a transformation in his character and relationship with God.

Isaiah's Vision of God's Throne: In Isaiah 6, the prophet Isaiah has a vision of God seated on a high and exalted throne, with seraphim surrounding Him and proclaiming, "Holy, holy, holy is the Lord Almighty; the whole earth is full of his glory" **[Isaiah 6:3]**. This sight overwhelms Isaiah, recognizing his unworthiness and sinfulness in the presence of a holy God. This vision leads to Isaiah's commissioning as a prophet, illustrating how a face-to-face encounter with God can lead to a profound sense of purpose and mission.

Paul's Encounter on the Road to Damascus: In the New Testament, one of the most dramatic encounters with God occurs on the road to Damascus. Saul, a zealous persecutor of Christians, suddenly sees a blinding light. He hears the voice of Jesus asking, "Saul, and Saul, why do you persecute me?" **[Acts 9:4]**. This encounter leads to Saul's conversion to Christianity and his transformation into Paul, one of the most influential apostles. It is a powerful example of how coming face to face with God can lead to radical change and a new direction in life.

Encounters with God are revelations of His holiness, glory, and love. These aspects of God's nature are central to understanding what it means to come face-to-face with Him. God's holiness is a recurring theme in the Bible, particularly in moments of divine encounter. To encounter God is to experience His absolute purity and moral perfection. In the story of Moses at the burning bush, God's command to remove his sandals emphasizes the sacredness of the encounter. Isaiah's vision of God's throne also underscores this holiness, leading the prophet to confess his unworthiness.

Holiness is not just an attribute of God but the essence of His being and it demands reverence and awe from those who encounter it.

God's glory is another crucial aspect revealed in divine encounters. Glory, in the biblical sense, refers to God's weighty and majestic presence. In **Exodus 33:18-23,** Moses asks to see God's glory. God agrees to pass by Moses, but He shields Moses from seeing His face directly, as "no one may see me and live" **[Exodus 33:20].** This passage illustrates the overwhelming power and majesty of God's presence, which is too intense for human eyes to behold fully. Yet, even a glimpse of God's glory can affect a person's life.

While God's holiness and glory might inspire fear and reverence, His love draws people closer to Him. The encounters with God often reveal His love and desire for intimacy with humanity. In the New Testament, Jesus embodies this love, offering Himself as a way for humanity to have a direct relationship with God. **John 1:14** states, "The Word became flesh and made his dwelling among us. We have seen his glory, the glory of the one and only Son, who came from the Father, full of grace and truth." Jesus is the ultimate revelation of God's love, showing that coming face to face with God is not just about experiencing His holiness and glory but also His deep, sacrificial love.

Encounters with God are not merely mystical experiences but transformative events that can change a person's life. These encounters often lead to a deeper understanding of one's purpose, a more significant commitment to God's will, and a profound change in character.

A New identity and purpose.

Many biblical figures who encountered God gave them new identities and purposes. For example, Jacob's encounter with God changed his name to Israel and marked him as the father of a nation. Similarly, Saul's transformation accompanied a new mission to spread the Gospel to the Gentiles. These examples show that coming face-to-face with God often leads to rediscovering who we are and our calling.

Deepened faith and commitment.

Encountering God can also deepen one's faith and commitment. After his encounter at the burning bush, Moses became a leader who guided the Israelites out of Egypt and through the wilderness. After his vision of God, Isaiah dedicated his life to proclaiming God's message to the people of Israel. These individuals were imperfect, but their encounters with God gave them the faith and strength to carry out their divine missions.

We cannot casually demonstrate faith and commitment to God. Faith and commitment is a condition of the heart. We demonstrate faith through our commitment to trust God even when we do not understand.

Transformation of character.

Divine encounters often lead to significant changes in a person's character. Jacob, whose brothers labeled his deceitfulness, became Israel, a man who wrestled with God and prevailed. Paul, who was once a persecutor of Christians, became one of the most passionate apostles of Christ. These transformations are a testament to the power of God's presence to change hearts and lives.

Encountering God has profound implications for how we live our lives. These encounters call us to live in a way that reflects God's holiness, glory, and love, and they challenge us to respond to His presence with reverence, obedience, and devotion. Encountering God's holiness and glory should lead us to live in reverence and awe of Him. **Proverbs 9:10** states, "The fear of the Lord is the beginning of wisdom, and knowledge of the Holy One understands." This "fear" is not about fear of God but deep respect and reverence for His majesty and power. It means recognizing that God is holy and that our lives should reflect that holiness in how we live, think, and act.

Divine encounters often come with a call to obedience. When God reveals Himself, He usually also reveals His will for our lives. God assigned Moses to lead the Israelites out of Egypt, commissioned Isaiah as a prophet, and sent Paul to preach to the Gentiles. Obedience to God's will is a natural response to encountering His presence. It involves submitting our plans and desires to God and trusting His ways are higher than ours [Isaiah 55:9].

Encountering God should inspire a life of devotion and worship. This devotion is about religious rituals and a wholehearted commitment to God in every aspect of life. **Romans 12:1** urges believers, "Therefore, I urge you, brothers and sisters, given God's mercy, to offer your bodies as a living sacrifice, holy and pleasing to God—this is your true and proper worship." A life of devotion means offering every part of ourselves to God, living in a way that honors Him in all we do.

While encountering God is a transformative experience, we cannot manufacture or force it. God often initiates these encounters and comes in His timing and way. However, certain attitudes and practices can prepare us to be receptive to God's presence. Humility is essential in seeking an encounter with God. **James 4:6-8** says, "God opposes the proud but shows favor to the humble. Submit yourselves, then, to God. Resist the devil, and he will flee from you. Come near to God, and he will come near to you." Humility involves recognizing our need for God and admitting it.

As George, Richard, Susan, and Cathy sat together, reflecting on their individual and collective journeys, a profound realization began to dawn on them. Each of them had faced challenges, doubts, and moments of feeling lost, yet through it all, they could now see how God had been orchestrating their paths toward this very moment. George spoke first, his voice filled with awe. "All this time, we've been searching—for purpose, answers, and peace—but God truly wanted us to encounter Him. Not just to know about Him, but to know Him intimately." Richard nodded, his eyes glistening. "I see it now," he said. "Every struggle, every detour, even the moments of silence, were God's way of drawing us closer to Him. He's revealed His heart to us, shaping our souls to align with His will."

Susan and Cathy exchanged glances, both deeply moved. Susan leaned forward, her voice trembling with emotion. "What God wants isn't about what we do or achieve—it's about surrender. He's shown us that true fulfillment comes from letting Him fill every part of our being." Cathy added softly, "It's like He's been peeling back the layers of our hearts to reveal the truth we've been too blind to see: He is enough. His revelations aren't just for guidance—they're for transformation." Together, they realized their journey was not about reaching a destination but discovering God in every step. In that sacred moment, they committed to embracing God's revelations, letting His truth lead their souls into deeper communion with Him.

Discovering God in every step of our lives is not a one-time event but a continual journey of faith. God is not distant or detached from the details of our lives; He is intimately involved in every moment, every decision, and every challenge we face. To discover God, we must learn to see His presence in the mundane and the extraordinary. Whether at work, spending time with family, or facing a difficult circumstance, God is there, guiding, teaching, and transforming us. By cultivating an awareness of His constant presence, we can experience His peace, wisdom, and direction in all our lives.

The key to discovering God in every step is to build a habit of seeking Him daily. This starts with intentional time spent in prayer, asking God to open our eyes to His presence and leading. As we immerse ourselves in Scripture, we understand more deeply who God is and how He moves in our lives. In moments of stillness, we become attuned to His voice, discerning His guidance in the small and major decisions. When we actively invite God into each part of our day, we create space for His Holy Spirit to speak to us, lead us in the right direction, and show us how He works in our circumstances.

Moreover, discovering God in every step of our lives requires a heart open to His purposes. Life is often unpredictable, and we may not always understand the reasons behind our challenges. However, when we trust that God is working all things together for our good (Romans 8:28), we begin to see that each step, even the difficult ones, has a divine purpose. Whether through lessons learned, character development, or opportunities for growth, God uses every experience to draw us closer to Him and to shape us into who He has called us to be. As we walk in faith and rely on His guidance, we come to know Him more deeply, and our lives reflect His love, wisdom, and grace to the world around us.

CHAPTER 20

REVELATIONS FOR THE SOUL

The revelations for the soul involve deep, spiritual insights and truths that God unveiled to individuals. These revelations often pertain to understanding one's purpose, identity, and destiny within God's divine plan. Throughout the Bible, we see numerous instances where God reveals profound truths to individuals, shedding light on their spiritual journey and guiding them toward a closer relationship with Him.

Susan and Cathy returned home and saw George and Richard sitting on the patio. They did not want to disturb them. Therefore, they went into the Family Room to relax and chat. "This has been a marvelous journey," Susan said to Cathy. "I agree, Susan. We have witnessed a great transformation with our husband. They are not the same two men," Cathy responded. Cathy and Susan witnessed what happens when they fully comprehend the God of the Bible. Religion created a God of the church that is unlike the God of the Bible. The God of the Bible works to transform us into the image of Christ – the Son of God. The church works to transform us into denominational doctrines, complete reliance on the Pastor, and assessments of the church based on how we feel. We left feeling strong. Unfortunately, it is a mistruth. The first time a storm arises in our lives, we fall apart.

George and Richard came into the Family. "Glad to see you ladies made it home safely. Richard and my eyes are fully open now. God's purpose for His word is to give us revelations for our souls. His desire is for us to develop our souls. The spirit of man or our mind is not what He's working on. He's working on establishing a character consistent with His," George said. "Yes, God's character is consistent. He will never change. He gives us a part of Him by the Holy Spirit and deposits us. At our death, He removes that part of Him from us and returns it to Himself," Richard said. "Tell us more, Gentlemen. Looks like you have undercover more revelations while we were busy taking care of things," Susan said. George smiled and looked at Richard. "Will you do the honors, Richard, and share the revelations for our soul with our favorite two people?" George asked.

Revelations of the soul serve several vital purposes in a believer's life. They are not random occurrences but intentional, divinely orchestrated moments that lead to a deeper understanding of God, oneself, and one's place in the world. One of the primary purposes of revelations is to reveal God's will and purpose for an individual's life. This can be seen in the story of Samuel in **1 Samuel 3**, where God calls out to the young boy in the middle of the night, revealing His plans for Samuel's future as a prophet. This profoundly personal revelation sets Samuel on a path of spiritual leadership and establishes a profound relationship between him and God. Similarly, in the New Testament, Paul's encounter with Jesus on the road to Damascus **[Acts 9]** is a revelation that radically changes the course of his life, revealing his new purpose as an apostle to the Gentiles. With their unique and personal nature, these personal revelations make us feel deeply connected and valued in God's plan, cherishing our integral role in His divine design.

Revelations often serve to deepen our understanding of who God is. In the Book of Job, for example, Job experiences intense suffering and wrestles with understanding God's justice and goodness. Through a divine revelation, God speaks to Job out of a whirlwind **[Job 38-41],** and Job gains a deeper understanding of God's sovereignty and wisdom. While not providing all the answers Job sought, this revelation transforms his perspective, leading him to greater humility and trust in God's character. It is a powerful reminder of the transformative power of divine revelations, inspiring us to remain hopeful and open to God's guidance.

Revelations can also reveal truths about one's identity and destiny. In Matthew 16:13-20, when Jesus asks His disciples who they think He is, Peter responds, "You are the Messiah, the Son of the living God." Jesus then reveals to Peter that God gave him this insight, not human understanding. This revelation confirms Peter's knowledge of Jesus' identity and shows Peter's role in the early church, as Jesus declares, "And I tell you that you are Peter, and on this rock, I will build my church" **[Matthew 16:18].** Such revelations help believers understand their unique role within God's plan and affirm their identity as children of God, instilling a deep sense of security and confidence in their purpose and reinforcing their place in the divine order.

Divine revelations often provide guidance and direction, especially during uncertainty or decision-making. In the Old Testament, Joseph, son of Jacob, receives a series of dreams **[Genesis 37]** that foretell his future and the role he will play in saving his family during a famine. Though these revelations initially lead to misunderstanding and hardship, they ultimately guide Joseph in fulfilling his God-given purpose. Similarly, in the New Testament, the Apostle Paul receives guidance through visions and revelations that direct his missionary journeys (Acts 16:9-10), ensuring that he follows God's plan for spreading the Gospel. This role of revelations in providing guidance reassures believers and instills confidence in their decisions, knowing they follow God's plan.

Revelations often serve as a source of encouragement and strength during challenging times. In the Book of Revelation, the Apostle John receives a series of visions that reveal the ultimate victory of Christ over evil. These revelations intend to strengthen and encourage believers facing persecution, reminding them of their hope in Christ's return and the establishment of God's kingdom. This is echoed in Paul's words in **2 Corinthians 12:1-10,** where he speaks of a "thorn in the flesh" and how, despite his suffering, he received a revelation from God that His grace is sufficient, which gave Paul the strength to endure his trials.

God's approach of revealing deep spiritual insights and truths to individuals, often called "revelations for the soul," serves a profound and intentional purpose. Revelations are not just for the sake of knowledge or information; they are for transformation. God desires to bring His people into a deeper understanding of His nature, His plans, and their identity in Him. These insights penetrate beyond the surface level, reaching the soul and heart of an individual because true spiritual growth comes from a place of internal renewal. When God reveals His truths, they are not simply meant to inform the mind but to change the heart, shaping us into the likeness of Christ and aligning our lives with His divine will.

One reason God uses this method is that He understands the depth of our need for personal encounters with Him. In a world filled with distractions and noise, losing sight of God's purpose for our lives is easy. God knows that for true transformation to occur, it must come from a personal relationship with Him, where His voice is heard clearly, and His presence is felt deeply. Revelations often come in moments of stillness when we are open and receptive to His guidance. This approach allows us to move past superficial religious practices and into a deeper intimacy with God. Through these personal revelations, God speaks directly to our hearts, teaching us about His character and our role in His eternal plan. They are tailored to where we are in our spiritual journey, providing wisdom, encouragement, and correction when necessary.

Furthermore, God uses revelations for the soul to strengthen our faith and equip us for the unique purposes He ordained for us. When God unveils a deeper truth or insight, it often brings clarity and direction to areas of our lives that may have been uncertain or unclear. These revelations become foundational in our walk with Him, empowering us to face challenges with confidence and obedience. As we learn to hear His voice more clearly and discern His will more accurately, we become more effective in fulfilling His calling on our lives. Through revelations, God invites us into a deeper partnership with Him, allowing us to be vessels of His love, wisdom, and purpose to the world around us. Ultimately, God uses this approach to draw us closer to Him, transform our hearts, and lead us toward the abundant life He has promised.

The benefits of revelations of the soul.

Revelations of the soul offer numerous benefits to believers, contributing to their spiritual growth, personal development, and deeper relationship with God. Revelations are instrumental in promoting spiritual growth and maturity. As believers receive divine insights, they must grow in their faith and understanding of God's word. This process often involves refining one's character and developing extraordinary patience, humility, and dependence on God. **Hebrews 5:12-14** speaks of the importance of moving beyond elementary teachings and growing into spiritual maturity, often facilitated by divine revelations that deepen our understanding of God's truths. Revelations can lead to significant personal transformation as individuals confront divine truths that challenge their thinking and living. In **Romans 12:2,** Paul urges believers, "Do not conform to the pattern of this world but be transformed by renewing your mind. Then you can test and approve God's will—his good, pleasing, and perfect will." Revelations play a crucial role in this renewal process, providing the insights needed to align one's life more closely with the will of God.

While divine revelations can significantly increase a believer's faith and trust in God, it is essential to acknowledge that they can also be a source of confusion or doubt for some. Discerning whether a revelation is genuinely from God can be challenging, and sometimes, we misinterpret or misapply a revelation. However, when God tangibly reveals His plans, character, or presence, it can reassure the believer of His faithfulness and sovereignty. This is evident in the life of Abraham, who received multiple revelations from God regarding his descendants and the Promised Land **[Genesis 12, 15, 17].** Despite the seemingly impossible circumstances, these revelations strengthened Abraham's faith, leading him to trust God's promises even when they were not immediately fulfilled **[Romans 4:18-21].**

Revelations often empower believers for service and mission. When God reveals His purposes, He equips individuals with the strength, wisdom, and resources needed to fulfill their calling. This can be seen in the life of the prophet Jeremiah, who received a revelation of his calling to be a prophet to the nations even before he was born **[Jeremiah 1:4-10]**. Despite his initial reluctance and challenges, Jeremiah was empowered by this revelation to fulfill his prophetic mission. Revelations contribute to greater discernment and wisdom, helping believers navigate life's complexities with divine insight. **James 1:5** encourages believers to ask God for wisdom, promising He will give generously to those seeking it. Divine revelations are often how this wisdom is imparted, enabling believers to make decisions that align with God's will and purpose. This enhanced discernment is crucial for living a life that honors God and fulfills His plans.

Perhaps the most significant benefit of revelations is the more profound intimacy with God that they foster. When God reveals Himself to an individual, it creates a profound connection between the believer and the Creator. This intimacy is evident in the relationship between Moses and God, as described in **Exodus 33:11: "The Lord would speak to Moses face to face, as one speaks to a friend."** Such revelations lead to a closer, more personal relationship with God, where the believer feels known, loved, and guided by the Creator.

God spoke to Moses face to face to establish a unique and direct relationship with Moses, who served as the leader and mediator for the people of Israel. This close communication was essential for Moses to receive clear guidance, instruction, and laws from God, particularly regarding the covenant between God and Israel. By speaking face to face, God provided Moses with detailed knowledge of His will, allowing Moses to lead the people with authority and divine insight.

This encounter also highlighted Moses' unique role as a prophet and leader, distinguished by his deep intimacy with God, which set him apart from others. It emphasized the importance of direct divine revelation in guiding the Israelites toward their destiny and fulfilling God's plan. The face-to-face interaction symbolized transparency, trust, and Moses's profound responsibility in conveying God's message to His people.

Direct divine revelation plays a crucial role in religious traditions, serving as how God or a higher power communicates essential truths, guidance, and wisdom to humanity. It offers an unmediated and authoritative source of spiritual knowledge, bypassing human interpretation or distortion. Throughout history, figures such as Moses, prophets, and apostles received direct revelations that shaped religious doctrines and clarified divine will. These revelations are foundational for faith communities, as they confirm the presence of the sacred and serve as a guide for moral, ethical, and spiritual living.

In many traditions, direct divine revelation is a way for believers to understand their purpose, responsibilities, and relationship with the divine. It establishes a personal connection between God and those who receive it, affirming that the sacred is actively involved in the lives of individuals and the world. Through these revelations, recipients often receive unique insights or instructions meant to benefit not just them but entire communities. As seen with Moses, direct revelation established essential laws and principles that governed the Israelites, forming the core of their covenant with God.

Moreover, direct divine revelation provides a sense of certainty and authority that other forms of spiritual or religious knowledge might lack. Because it comes directly from a higher power, we must view revelations as infallible and beyond question, affecting religious teachings, practices, and beliefs. This certainty empowers religious leaders and prophets to speak with confidence and conviction, knowing they convey messages directly from God. In this way, divine revelation guides individual behavior and shapes the direction of entire religious movements, helping believers navigate the complexities of life and faith.

As George, Richard, Cathy, and Susan sat in reflective silence, the weight of their shared experiences settled into profound clarity. Almost simultaneously, their eyes lit up with understanding, and George broke the silence. "It's not about what we've been chasing," he said, his voice tinged with awe. "It's about what God has been trying to reveal to us all along—truths that transform our souls." Cathy nodded, her voice filled with emotion. "He's not just giving us answers to our questions; He's giving us revelations that shape who we are, that deepen our connection with Him." Richard added, "It's not about fixing the circumstances around us but about letting Him renew what's inside us." Smiling through tears, Susan whispered, "All this time, He's been after our hearts, showing us that His revelations are meant to bring us closer to Him and into the people He created us to be." In that moment, they felt a collective "aha," a spiritual awakening that filled them with peace and purpose.

When we approach God with questions, seeking answers to the complexities of our lives, it is easy to assume that He will provide clear, direct responses to our specific inquiries. We often bring our questions about our future, our relationships, or the difficulties we face, hoping for a precise solution or a systematic guide. However, God does not always answer our questions through direct answers. Instead, He often gives us revelations—deeper spiritual truths and insights—that do not necessarily answer our questions directly but shape who we are and deepen our connection with Him. These revelations are not merely about gaining information; they are about transformation. They change how we see ourselves, our circumstances, and, most importantly, our relationship with God.

God's revelations are designed to reach the heart of who we are. While we may ask about circumstances, outcomes, or struggles, God sees deeper into our hearts, knowing that what we need most is not always an answer but a deeper understanding of His character, ways, and will. Revelations often reveal something within us that needs attention or a deeper truth about God that we have yet to comprehend fully. For example, when we ask God, "Why am I facing this hardship?" He may not immediately provide the specific answer we desire. Still, He may instead reveal something about His nature—His faithfulness, sovereignty, and love—that helps us endure with peace and trust, even without understanding every detail of the situation. Through these revelations, we learn to rely more on who God is than on the answers we think we need.

In Scripture, many of the greatest spiritual leaders were not given immediate answers to their questions but were given revelations that reshaped their understanding of God and their calling. Consider Moses at the burning bush. Moses' first question to God was, "Who am I that I should go to Pharaoh and bring the Israelites out of Egypt?" (Exodus 3:11). Instead of offering Moses a list of reasons why he was the right person for the job, God revealed His name to Moses—"I AM WHO I AM" (Exodus 3:14). This revelation did not answer Moses' question directly but pointed Moses back to the eternal, self-sufficient nature of God. It was not about Moses' abilities or qualifications but about the power and presence of God that would accompany him. In that moment, Moses' perspective shifted from his inadequacies to God's sovereignty, and his faith was deepened.

Similarly, when the Apostle Paul asked God to remove the "thorn in his flesh," a persistent struggle or affliction, God's response was not a direct answer but a profound revelation: "My grace is sufficient for you, for my power is made perfect in weakness" (2 Corinthians 12:9). Paul did not get the answer he was looking for. Still, he was given a revelation that reshaped his approach to suffering. Instead of seeking a way out of his pain, Paul understood that God's grace and power were most evident in his weakness. This revelation did not just answer his question—it transformed his understanding of God's work and empowered him to persevere with joy and humility.

God's revelations are also deeply personal. When seeking answers, we often focus on the specifics of our situation—how things will turn out, what we should do next, and why things are happening the way they are. However, God's answer to us is often about something much deeper than the immediate circumstances. It is about our hearts, trust in Him, and willingness to surrender to His will. These revelations are not just intellectual answers; they are encounters with the living God that shift our priorities, increase our faith, and deepen our love for Him. Through revelations, God invites us into a relationship with Him where trust, not just knowledge, is the foundation of our walk with Him.

For example, when we face a difficult decision, God may not immediately give us a clear "yes" or "no" answer. Instead, He may reveal more about His character—showing us His faithfulness, goodness, and wisdom. This deeper understanding of God can shape our decision-making process, helping us to act with more confidence, peace, and trust in His guidance. The revelation of who God is becomes the lens through which we view our circumstances, changing how we respond to challenges. This process of spiritual growth, shaped by revelations, gradually transforms our hearts and minds, leading us to live more in alignment with God's will.

The purpose of God's revelations is not to satisfy our curiosity or answer our immediate questions but to bring us closer to His heart. God desires to transform us from the inside out, shaping our character, deepening our connection with Him, and empowering us to live out our purpose in the world. Revelations help us see things through God's eyes, giving us eternal perspectives beyond the temporary circumstances we may be focused on. As we receive and respond to these divine insights, we begin to live more fully in God's peace, trust His timing, and embrace His plan, even when we do not have all the answers. This journey of discovering God's revelations is not just about finding answers but about becoming more like Christ, reflecting His love, wisdom, and grace to the world around us.

CHAPTER 20

THE NEXT CHAPTER

God's ultimate desire for His people is to bring them closer to Himself and guide them into the fullness of life He has planned for them. This journey of growth and transformation often involves moving from one chapter of our lives to the next. However, God does not simply push us forward into the unknown without preparation. Instead, He offers revelations for our souls to prepare us for the next chapter, revelations that align with His perfect will and purpose. These divine insights shape our hearts, shift our perspectives, and provide the spiritual foundation to move forward with faith, confidence, and clarity.

In many ways, these revelations are the divine "pointers" that guide us in the direction God wants us to go. However, they are not always about clear, systematic instructions for the future. More often than not, God uses revelations to deepen our understanding of His character, love, and plans, preparing us for the next season by transforming us from the inside out. The spiritual insights God designs to challenge, refine, and equip us with the wisdom, strength, and peace we need to navigate the unknowns of the next chapter. As we grow in our knowledge of God and our relationship with Him, He gradually prepares us for what lies ahead. Our hearts become aligned with His will, our trust in Him deepens, and we become more confident in His ability to lead us wherever He wants us to go.

One of the key purposes of these revelations is to build our faith and trust in God. When we face transitions—whether in relationships, careers, or personal growth—it is easy to be filled with doubt and fear about the future. We may feel uncertain about the direction we are meant to take, or we may be afraid of the challenges ahead. However, God desires to reveal His presence and faithfulness more profoundly in these moments. Revelations are not just for our understanding—they are for our transformation. For example, when uncertain about a major life decision, God may not immediately give us a clear "yes" or "no" answer. Instead, He might reveal something about His faithfulness or perfect timing, reminding us that He is in control and that we can trust Him with every detail of our lives. These insights build our trust in God and help us to surrender our plans, knowing that His plans are always better and that He will guide us to the next chapter at the right time.

God's revelations also help clarify our future purpose and direction. As we move from one chapter to the next, it is important to understand that each season has a unique purpose. God has been shaping us through every experience; those lessons are building blocks for what He has in store. The revelations He gives us reveal parts of His purpose for us, helping us see how our past, present, and future interconnect with His divine plan. These revelations often challenge us to let go of past hurts, disappointments, or fears so we can step boldly into what God has for us next. They remind us that the past does not define our future and that God is constantly at work, weaving together every detail of our lives for His glory. By receiving these revelations, we can embrace the next chapter with a deeper sense of purpose and a clearer understanding of how God calls us to serve Him and others in this new season.

God's revelations help us move forward with peace and assurance, even in the face of uncertainty. Transitions can be stressful, and we often feel overwhelmed by the unknowns. Nevertheless, God's revelations bring clarity and calm to our souls. When we understand that God is not just leading us unquestioningly but actively revealing His will and purposes for us, we can confidently move forward. These insights help us see the bigger picture, reminding us that God controls the journey, even when the path seems unclear. Revelations for the soul enable us to trust in God's timing, knowing He will not lead us into a new chapter without equipping us with the challenges and opportunities it will bring.

Receiving and responding to these revelations is crucial for our spiritual maturity. It is easy to feel stuck or uncertain during times of transition, but it is during these moments that God is often trying to do His most significant work in us. As we seek Him, He gives us the revelations to grow spiritually, develop emotionally, and step into the next chapter of our lives with faith and trust. These revelations shape our character, give us clarity of vision, and prepare us to fulfill God's purpose in this new season. They help us grow in wisdom and understanding so we can move forward not with fear or hesitation but with confidence in the One leading us.

Ultimately, God's revelations for our souls invite us to trust Him more fully and embrace His plan for the next chapter of our lives. Receiving these insights is not always easy; it often requires a willingness to surrender our ideas and plans, but the reward is a deeper relationship with God and a clearer understanding of our path forward. As we seek God for wisdom and guidance, He will reveal exactly what we need to know in His perfect timing. These revelations are gifts of grace, not just for understanding but also for transformation. They empower us to step into the next chapter with a heart fully surrendered to God's will, ready to walk in His peace and purpose.

GGeorge, Richard, Susan, and Cathy's epiphany determined the following steps in their journey of discovery. After receiving divine revelation, the first and most crucial step is to seek a deeper understanding of the message. In the Bible, when prophets received messages from God, they often went into deep reflection. For instance, when Daniel received visions about the future, he prayed to God for understanding **[Daniel 9:2-3]**. Similarly, when Mary received the angel's message that she would give birth to the Messiah, she "pondered these things in her heart" **[Luke 2:19]**. Understanding the depth and scope of the message is necessary before we take any action. This process of reflection allows one to discern the meaning, purpose, and relevance of the revelation to one's life and situation.

After understanding the message, the next step is discerning its implications. Divine revelation often has practical, spiritual, and emotional consequences. God may reveal something that calls for personal change, repentance, or action. Other times, the message may provide encouragement, confirmation, or direction for future endeavors. Therefore, it is essential to understand how the revelation fits into the larger framework of one's life.

This step involves evaluating the current state of affairs, as the revelation might serve as an invitation to shift priorities or re-evaluate certain relationships, careers, or ministries. It is common for divine messages to challenge personal comfort zones, encouraging the recipient to grow in areas where they may have been stagnant or complacent. For instance, it required a radical change when God called Abraham to leave his homeland and go to a land he had never seen **[Genesis 12:1]**. It forced him to leave behind familiarity and security for an unknown future.

Discernment also includes understanding the timing and scope of the message. Not every revelation requires immediate action, but some may call for urgency. For example, when Joseph, the earthly father of Jesus, received the revelation in a dream that he should flee to Egypt to protect Jesus from Herod **[St. Matthew 2:13-14]**, the revelation came with a clear and immediate directive. In contrast, other revelations, such as prophetic visions, might unfold over time and require patience and preparation. Therefore, discerning the next steps involves carefully examining the timing, scope, and resources needed to act on the revelation.

In the process of growing in faith, we attune to the voice of God and more sensitive to the leading of the Holy Spirit. Wisdom is developed through experience—successes and failures—allowing the individual to approach future revelations with greater confidence, patience, and discernment. Spiritual growth also makes room for greater responsibility in the kingdom of God. As Jesus taught in the parable of the talents, those who are faithful with little, God will entrust with more **[St. Matthew 25:23].** In this way, revelation is not a singular event but part of an ongoing relationship with God that continually transforms the individual.

"These last few months have been incredible. The Holy Spirit led us in a way that we cannot reverse. We have to share this knowledge with Pastor Howell and our other friends," George said. "Yes, I am thinking about how many Sundays we sat at church trying to "get a word from the Lord and didn't realize that God's word grants us a revelation. God intends to give us revelations that can lead us to the next Chapter. In that next chapter, we go from faith to faith, "Richard said. Susan looked at George with teary eyes and said, "Thank you for sharing this with me. I have learned so much." "We all have, they responded."

The next chapter provides a road map for what to do when one receives a revelation. God grants us revelations to show us great and mighty things we do not know. However, the next chapter details God's leading by His Holy Spirit to help us achieve that divine nature in transforming into the image of Christ. .

The weight of their newfound understanding settled in as George, Richard, Susan, and Cathy sat together. The purpose of the revelations of the soul had become clear to them—these were not merely insights or answers to their questions; they were divine invitations to grow closer to God and align their lives with His will. "I feel like we've been given a map," George said thoughtfully, "but it's not about following it to some destination. It's about the journey and how we live it with God leading us." He paused, looking at the others. "Now that we understand this, what do we do with it? How do we apply these revelations to our lives?"

Richard, reflecting on the profound transformation they had experienced, spoke up. "I think it begins with surrender," he said. "We've spent so much of our lives trying to control the outcome and make things happen in our way. But now, we realize that God's will isn't about us achieving something—it's about yielding to His process and trusting Him every step of the way." He looked around at the group, his voice firm with conviction. "We need to live in a way responsive to God's whispers, letting His revelations guide our decisions, actions, and even our thoughts."

Susan nodded in agreement, adding, "It's also about deepening our relationship with God. They're not just truths we learn—they're truths that change us." She leaned in, her heart swelling with purpose. "It's about aligning with His will, not just in the big moments, but in the small, daily decisions."

Feeling the weight and beauty of it all, Cathy summed it up. "It's like we've been entrusted with something sacred," she said softly. "These revelations are not for us alone—they're meant to be shared. God wants to use us to help others experience the same transformation, to guide them to the deeper truths He's revealed to us." Her eyes sparkled with excitement. "This is just the beginning. We must take what we learned and walk it out with integrity, love, and compassion. Our lives now have a purpose on an entirely new level, and I believe this is precisely what God wants from us. "Let's meet next weekend and explore what the next chapter look like for us.

George, Susan, Cathy, and Richard gathered in the cozy living room of George and Susan's home, the aroma of freshly brewed coffee mingling with the sound of the crackling fireplace. The four friends had been journeying together for months, exploring spiritual truths and documenting their insights into their understanding of revelations for their souls. Their discussions had transformed their lives and deepened their faith, and now it was time to plan the next chapter.

"So," George began, looking around at his friends, "what do we feel God is leading us to explore next?" Susan, ever the reflective one, spoke up first. "I've been thinking about how we've touched on repentance and the role of the Holy Spirit, but we haven't delved into the concept of grace. What does it truly mean to live in God's grace? How do we avoid taking it for granted while also not living under the weight of guilt?" Her words hung in the air, resonating deeply with the group.

Cathy nodded thoughtfully. "That's a great point, Susan. Grace is a foundational part of our faith but is often misunderstood. Maybe we could look at how grace transforms not just our relationship with God but also our relationships with others. Imagine a section discussing extending grace to people in difficult circumstances. That could be powerful."

Richard leaned forward, his face lighting up with enthusiasm. "I love that idea. In addition, to build on it, what if we included a section about the intersection of grace and purpose? Once we understand God's grace, how does that empower us to step into His calling for us? I think many people struggle with feeling inadequate or unworthy of their purpose. Grace could be the key to unlocking that."

George smiled, jotting down notes as they spoke. "You're both onto something. Grace isn't just a theological concept; it's efficient. It changes how we see the world around us. Maybe we can structure the chapter into three parts: understanding grace, living in grace, and sharing grace. Each part could include Scripture, personal reflections, and practical applications."

"What about stories?" Cathy suggested. "People connect with stories. Maybe we could include testimonies or examples of how grace has affected real lives. We could even draw from our own experiences." Susan's eyes lit up. "Oh, I love that idea! In addition, it does not have to be our stories. We could invite others to contribute as well. Imagine the richness of hearing how God's grace has worked in diverse lives."

"Yes, and we could end the chapter with an invitation," Richard added. "An invitation for readers to reflect on their own experience with grace and to take a step toward embracing it more fully in their lives. Maybe include some guided questions or a prayer."

George looked around the room, his heart full. "This is it. I feel like God is leading us in the right direction. Grace is not just a topic—it is the heart of the gospel. This next chapter could change lives if we communicate even a fraction of its beauty and power."

As the evening wore on, the four friends continued to brainstorm, their conversation weaving together Scripture, personal insights, and practical ideas. By the time they wrapped up, they had a clear vision for the next chapter of *Revelations for the Soul* and a renewed sense of purpose for their journey. The warmth of their fellowship and the excitement of what lay ahead filled the room, a testament to the grace they were about to share with the world.

The next evening, George called the group together again, his notebook in hand and a thoughtful expression on his face. As they settled into their familiar seats, he posed a question that had been weighing on his heart. "When do we begin our journey into understanding this next chapter?" he asked, Susan leaned back, her fingers tapping the edge of her mug. "That's a powerful question, George. Maybe the journey begins now, with us intentionally seeking to embody grace in our own lives. If we are going to write about understanding and sharing grace, we need to experience it deeply ourselves. What if we set aside time each day to reflect, pray, and ask God to show us areas where we need to grow in grace?"- stay tuned for the next chapter.

www.ingramcontent.com/pod-product-compliance
Lightning Source LLC
LaVergne TN
LVHW081333060426
835513LV00014B/1269